Brussels: The Beer Capital

Beer Guide to the city

ISBN: 9798332944994

Second Edition

Copyright © Niccolò Querci

Contents

Foreword

by Andrea Turco[1]

At the beginning of the 2000s, I organised my first "beer trip" abroad, but I had no doubts about the destination; Belgium and in particular Brussels. At that time, the craft beer movement was still taking its first steps in Italy, and the products in high demand were Belgian. There were no reports on the web, of those who had been to Brussels to discover the traditional cafes of the city, or who had gone to visit the fascinating Cantillon, or dined in renowned restaurants with an exquisite "cuisine à la bière". My expectations were very high, and I was very enthusiastic.

I was not disappointed. Brussels immediately astonished me, and I was struck by how important beer was in the everyday life of its citizens. For me, it was like being suddenly catapulted into a giant amusement park, steeped in beer culture in every corner. The first hours spent in the centre, between the Grand Place and the Bourse, allowed me to visit historic beer places, beer shops offering so much, bistros with craft beer on draught. I was fascinated even to find the names Stella Artois and Jupiler at so many locations, despite being rather unremarkable commercial brands. But it was that ubiquitous presence of beer that happily left me speechless.

Over my few days in Brussels, I spent several hours in some old cafes — I remember with nostalgia the Zageman

---

[1] Freelance Consultant in the beer market – Lecturer – Judge – Event organizer – Founder of Cronache di Birra.

(now closed) and the Old Bier Circus (now transformed into a renowed beer restaurant). I visited the unmissable Cantillon brewery and tasted their extraordinary products, with brands dating back to former times. I also visited other cities, such as Ghent, Bruges and Antwerp, but the capital remained central to my short holiday on Belgian land.

After that first visit, I returned to Brussels at least a dozen times to participate as a judge in beer contests, or to take part in press trips. Over those years I have seen the city evolve, managing to maintain balance between tradition — and what tradition! — and modernity. In particular, Brussels is experiencing a new beer spring in recent times, with the opening of many small breweries arising from young, fresh and sometimes visionary projects. There has also been a change to the landscape; some historical premises are no longer in existence, while new cafes have opened marketing the new products.

I am sure that Brussels was not always the lively, dynamic, ever-changing beer city it is now. Many of the brands of Stella Artois and Jupiler have been replaced by those of De La Senne, the city brewery that paved the way for all the modern craft producers who arrived more recently. Unlike other classic beer destinations, Brussels has managed to enhance its brewing past without remaining exclusively tied to it. The city has managed to renew itself without denying its own traditions, indeed maintaining in many cases a shared thread between past and present. After years of being considered the capital of a beer culture now largely outdated, Brussels has become an essential destination now for every enthusiast.

For this very reason, the guidebook you have in your hands is a valuable tool to get to know Brussels breweries, but also to retrace the history of their recent development.

Niccolò has been living in the Belgian capital for several years and has considerable expertise in the field. This brings added value to his writing of this book as an enthusiastic lover of beer, a traveller who likes to find new breweries and interesting places, both in Brussels and in the rest of the world. It embodies the most authentic concept of "beer hunter", the one that the famous beer connaiseur, Michael Jackson invented and interpreted in an admirable way in his books on beer.

This work is the direct result of Niccolò's passion and interest in beer, an extraordinary work of lucidity and depth of content, from which all Niccolò's great passion for beer shines out.

This guide will be useful for anyone touring Brussels to sample beer, but it will also be enjoyable as a reference book thanks to some very interesting extra content. This was something that was missing in the literature dedicated to our beloved drink. I am happy that it was Niccolò who filled this gap. Enjoy it!

Introduction

I arrived in Brussels for the first time on 11 January 2011 to participate to the Erasmus Programme at the Université Libre of Brussels.

It was snowing and it was very cold. My French was not at all good, and indeed I have to admit that I knew very little about beer.

I did not arrive in Brussels with the myth of Gueuze, I was not aware of the existence of the Moeder Lambic, I had never participated in a real beer tasting event, and I had never tasted the iconic De Dolle's Stille Natch.

I was a young Italian guy living in Bergamo and attending university in Milan. My social life was rather dull and when I drank in a bar I invariably ordered ordinary industrial beers or watery cocktails.

It is quite likely that I had tasted a Chimay (or something similar) but the only thing that struck me, beyond the alcohol level, was the price; too high for the penniless student that I was.

Moreover, it was my first experience of living alone. Before that, my grandmother and my mother took care of all my needs (food, clothes). I needed to learn how to survive.

More than 10 years have passed since those first days. My life has changed greatly since then from many perspectives; work, love, leisure, but especially my knowledge of beer, the subject of this book.

My initial experience with Belgian beers was in many ways overwhelming. But it was not immediate because, as you can imagine, an Erasmus student usually does not drink correctly like a "Sommelier". My tastes and knowledge developed gradually but steadily.

At the beginning, I chose beers for the name or for the label. I was especially attracted by Trappist beers. I was amazed about how a beer so high in alcohol could be so much less expensive than an average industrial Italian pint of beer in an Italian bar.

Step by step, I learned to recognise beer styles and to appreciate their aroma and taste. I even started to appreciate the famous Cantillon Gueuze.

Gradually, my curiosity turned into passion. I forced every family member or friend who came to visit me in Brussels to enjoy a tour of my favourite places to drink a beer.

Remember that the average Italian man has not tasted anything different that a "Peroni with ice" and usually drinks a beer only when he orders a pizza.

Such people suddenly found themselves in a busy bar in the university district faced with one, or more, strong Belgian Trappist or Abbey beers. Most appreciated the experience and returned to repeat the adventure. A few never came back.

As time went on, I decided to learn more about my new passion; beer.

Like many people, I started to brew at home. However, I soon stopped due to lack of time and space. I decided to focus on developing my theoretical knowledge by reading many books, web articles, and consulting beer forums.

When I purchased a car, I start also to tour other Belgian cities and towns and many breweries.

I even decided to formalise my knowledge. I dedicated part of my first year of salary to finance weekend trips to London and Edinburgh to follow the "Beer Sommelier course" at the Beer&Cider Academy of London. Luckily, I had an extensive network of friends in both cities always available to host me and thus allowing me to save money. Finally, I did it. I became an official "Beer Sommelier".

After this important step for me, at least, I founded, together with a Belgian friend, my Beer club; "Beer Tasters Brussels". We organised several successful beer tastings and pairing beer&food events. Unfortunately, the Covid pandemic halted us. Now, we are slowly starting again.

In the meantime, I started to write articles about beer and beer travels for "Cronache di Birra", the most important Italian blog about craft beers founded by the Italian beer judge, Andrea Turco. This blog was to allow me and many Italian beer lovers approach this magic world.

Beer is not a job for me, it is a passion. I love my current job in one of the most important European Institutions and I wish to continue it.

However, my passion for beer is visceral. Beer tasting, reading about beers and visiting breweries or beer places is my main leisure pursuit.

That is why I have decided to put my ten years of knowledge of Brussels at the service of beer enthusiasts.

Brussels is a vibrant, multi-ethnic and multicultural city. It is relatively scarcely populated (about 1.2 million inhabitants) but rather extensive and with great economic and social contradictions. It is a city with different "dimensions". Alongside the classical Belgian capital, there is the growth of the "Brussels of the expats" (or the EU Bubble) and the "Arabic and Turkish Brussels" with their individual lifestyle, beliefs and flavours, perhaps eclipsing the old Brussels. These are two often parallel worlds who interact infrequently, and often in a problematic way. Yet the city is characterised by the constant presence of beer. In Brussels, you might drink beer anywhere; from the old town to the European Institutions district, from the Arab districts of Anderlecht and Molenbeek to the rich northwest suburbs.

Everyone drinks beer; young and old, men and women, Belgians and foreigners. The first thing you see coming to Brussels-Midi station or Zaventem airport is people drinking beer. On the other hand, it is the national drink and the product that makes the "Petit Pays" famous all over the world. And while in virtually every corner of Belgium you will find a brewery, in Brussels you will find every beer brewed in the country (and now also in Europe).

A real Beer Capital.

Methodology

This book (or beer guide) opens with a brief chapter dedicated to the history of beer in Brussels. Then there is a chapter dedicated to the 19 breweries established in the city. Among beer enthusiasts there is a fervent debate as to which breweries can or cannot be considered as "Bruxellois". I have chosen to define as a brewery "from Brussels", a brewery who produces most of its products on site. I interviewed almost all the brewers because, in addition to their brewery, I wanted to know their view of the future of beer in the city.

However, I also want to offer a complete overview of the beer scene of Brussels. For this reason, I have dedicated a chapter to all the other entities (Beer firms and gipsy brewers) that do not have their own site or still do not produce totally in the city.

The second part of this book, is dedicated to the the different neighbourhoods of Brussels. For each neighbourhood, you will find a dedicated chapter. Each chapter has a QR code linked to a google map and a "suggested beer tour".

The other chapters are dedicated to beer shops, beer restaurants, museums and beer-themed spas. There are also sections detailing where to drink at the airport and in city parks,

Brussels is not a city but a region (more precisely Brussels-Capital Region) but for convenience in the book I define it as a "city".

Every opinion or judgement is purely personal, as is the choice of the places mentioned. Enjoy it!

History of beer in Brussels

Belgium, along with Germany, the Czech Republic and the United Kingdom, is in the top four European brewing countries in terms of history and tradition.

There is evidence of beer consumption since the Roman Empire Age, and during Julius Caesar's campaigns.

In the Middle Age, the production of beer became the prerogative of Christian monasteries. At the time, water was not drinkable. In fact, by drinking water there was a high probability of contracting disease. Many people, therefore, including monks and children, drank a light table beer. Although this was perhaps not quite appreciated at the time, the brewing process eliminated most of the germs. Once the beer was brewed, the monks added a mixture of herbs called "gruit" or hops, which served as an effective preservative. The Gruithuis (places managed by the Church that distributed the Gruit) were very important institutions.

In Brussels, the first historic fact relating to beer was the construction of the "Maison des Brasseurs" in 1522. This was later destroyed during a siege by the French in 1695.

By the end of the seventeenth century, the Brussels brewers were so rich and powerful that they could afford to build one of the most impressive buildings of the Grand Place; the "Maison de la Corporation des Brasseurs" built in 1698. The "Guild of Brewers" was an actual corporation to which it was very difficult, and very expensive, to become part of.

At that time, most of the breweries were family-run. For decades, the brewery trade was handed down from father to son. The entire family was involved in the production process. The sons and daughters of brewers tended to marry each other so that this trade remained a closed profession for a long time.

During the seventeenth and eighteenth centuries in Brussels, the most important beer styles in Brussels were Lambic, Faro and styles which have since disappeared such as Uytzet, Diestse, Hoegaerds and Peeterman.

At the beginning of the 18th century, in Brussels there were about 120 breweries located along or near the River Senne. At this time, the water was still clear and clean and was used to clean the installations. Water for brewing was taken from sources or wells.

During the French Revolution (1792-1794), the guilds were suppressed, and everyone was again free to brew beer on their own behalf. The number of breweries began to rise again, and in 1816 a new tax was introduced, based on the content of fermentation vats.

In 1822, a law amended excise duties on beer production. The calculation of excise duties was calculated on the basis of production capacity and no longer the quantity produced.

To overcome the increase in taxes, Belgian producers therefore increase the yield of their production to produce 60 hectolitres from a plant of 20 hectolitres. The beer then fermented faster but was also less alcoholic and more liquefied. It was simply not as good or as drinkable.

Consumers began to prefer German and English products. These products were stronger in alcohol. Foreign beers at the time were considered as "luxury products".

Another law of August 20, 1885, called the "Systermans Law" or "New Brewery Law", amended the law of 1822 and determined that excise duties should be calculated both on the amount of malt declared and on the capacity of the fermenter. This allowed brewers to choose alternative production methods and favoured the production of different styles which up to that moment were underrepresented; such as helles, pilsen or stout.

A very important figure of the 19th century Brussels was the "beer merchants".

There were about a hundred beer merchants in the city. The function of these merchants was to collect beer from brewers, especially Lambic and Mars (a mix of Lambic wheat and malted barley) and blend it in order to supply taverns and cabarets. Very often, these blends were sweetened or coloured.

Year after year, breweries located in what is now the city centre closed or gradually moved towards the periphery.

The first cause of this phenomenon is to be found in the events that characterised the last quarter of the eighteenth century. The industrial revolution was also underway in Belgium. Many industries used the waters of the Senne. This, combined with an increase in the population, caused strong pollution of the waters, making them unusable for breweries.

In 1806, only 29 breweries were still active in the city centre. The municipal administration opted to cover the river, which had become an open-air sewer, by constructing large avenues in the period between 1867 and 1872. After this work, only 14 breweries remained on site.

Other factors that caused the closure or the transfer out of the city of many breweries were the abolition of measures such as the "Octroi" (1860), and the customs tolls on the roads.

Therefore, an exodus of breweries to the suburbs began, particularly near the Brussels-Charleroi Canal and in the areas close to the new railway stations. With the change of location, the styles of brewed beer also began to change.

By 1850 the import of foreign beer styles was practically non-existent, and the beers brewed in Brussels were of three categories: Lambic, Gueuze and Faro.

With the approach of the new century, Pils started to be very competitive. Local producers initially reacted by continuing to produce Gueuze. But in a short time, Brussels Lambic producers (unlike those in Payotteland region) started brewing Export, Bock and Pils beers.

Quite quickly Pils beer style became more in demand. Particularly well known and popular beers were Forst of the Wielemans-Ceuoppens brewery, Canette of the Phoenix brewery, Elberg of the Grande Brasserie de Koekelberg, Primus of Brasserie Royale in Laeken, Star of Brasserie Leopold, Vox of Brasserie Chasse royale, Pearl of Caulier brewery and EKLA of the Vandenheuvel brewery.

In order to brew Pils, Brussels breweries had to switch to low fermentation processes. This required huge investments that not all breweries could afford. Many breweries merged with survive, others failed, or were absorbed by larger breweries.

At the beginning of the 20th century, Brussels had almost 86 breweries. 18 of these were in the city centre and 68 in the other municipalities of Brussels.

The 20th century, however, marked the decline of breweries in Brussels. The need to increase production pushed by the industrialisation process, caused the failure of many small breweries.

The First World War exacerbated the situation causing shortages of labour and raw materials. The Germans occupied Brussels, seized the horses (used to transport beer and initially replaced with cows) and then the copper with which the fermentation vats were made.

The economic crisis of the 1930s and World War II provided a fatal blow to the city brewing scene. In the second half of the twentieth century only the large breweries survived in Brussels and they gradually acquired the smaller ones.

Belgian beer production was put under intense pressure by German, Danish and English industrial beers. Local trade on which many breweries survived, suffered a deadly blow with the arrival of supermarkets. Cafes also began to sign exclusive contracts for the supply of beers with large breweries.

People's tastes also changed; industrial lagers were preferred to Lambic and Gueuze, leading to the closure of almost all breweries producing this style.

In 1949, the historic Brasserie Atlas was acquired by Brouwerij Haacht who in 1952 took its production out of Brussels.

The year of the Universal Exhibition in Brussels (whose Atomium is the most famous landmark), 1958, was the "Swan song" for the Brussels breweries. In exchange for substantial funding, a cartel of 32 Belgian breweries (several of them from Brussels) took control of the forty bars of the exhibition, making Belgian beers known to the world.

The 1969 was the "Annus horribilis" for the Brussels breweries; the Brasserie De Boeck was acquired by Belle-Vue, the Grande Brasserie de Koekelberg was bought and immediately closed by its historic rival, Brasserie Vandenheuvel, which in turn was acquired the following year by the English brewery Watneys who closed it five years later.

Moreover, several breweries were expropriated to make way for infrastructure projects; the brasserie Le Château d'Or which in 1968 was demolished to make way for the Ring in the south of the city while the Brasserie Leopold in 1981 made way for the current Spaak building of the European Parliament.

In 1988, the Brasserie Wielemans-Ceuppens (under the control of Artois since 1978) in the municipality of Forest, closed its doors. It was one of the largest and most modern in Europe when it was built in the 1930s,

In the 1990s, except for the AB Inbev brewery of BelleVue (active in Molenbeek until 2008), Brasserie Cantillon was the only brewery operating in Brussels. It remained the only one until 2010, when Brasserie de la

Senne opened, except for the brief experience of Brasserie de l'Imprimerie which had opened in Uccle in 2003.

Sadly, the architectural heritage of the Brussels breweries has almost totally disappeared, swallowed up by apartments, lofts, offices and storage sites. The most famous, the Brasserie Wielemans-Ceuppens is today a location for events, and there you can still admire the production vats.

Estaminet and Cafés

In the 19th century Brussels, there was a clear division between "Estaminet" and "Cafes".

The "Cafe", born in Vienna and later spread to the rest of Europe, was the reference point for the bourgeoisie who went there to debate, read newspapers, or just gather news.

The etymology of the term "Estaminet" dates back to the medieval Brabancon cabaret where it indicated a place to go to drink, smoke and eat.

The "Estaminet" in the nineteenth century was the favourite place of the working classes. There were many estaminets in the working-class neighbourhoods, while they were almost entirely absent from the wealthier neighbourhoods.

An estaminet was mostly frequented by men (only on Sundays were there families) and had an important social, cultural and recreational role. It was also a place of political propaganda.

In 1828, there was a very marked disproportion between estaminet and cafes. According to "Les Tablette Bruxelloise" there were 600 estaminets and only 4 cafes.

The concept of "Estaminet" got into difficulty by the end of the nineteenth century due to the profound change in the character of the city and a general change of mentality.

Many estaminets turned into cafes. By the end of the 19th century, there were 272 cafes, making the social distinction between the two types of premises more fluid and less marked.

The situation changed further in the twentieth century, or even more after the First World War. The concentration of places to drink beer in Brussels in 1930 was about one to every 100 inhabitants.

The Cafes were located in the most prestigious streets and were frequented by both men and women of the bourgeois class.

Morning was the time when men went there to conduct their business. In the afternoon, cafes were enjoyed by women who met their friends, while in the evening the cafes were patronised by couples who came to have a drink before or after a theatre show. More and more cafe customers ordered foreign beers, in particular Pils from Germany.

Estaminets customers were loyal to Gueuze and Faro, the typical beers of Brussels. Men went to estaminets mainly at the end of their work shift, or on Sunday afternoons with their family. They went there to drink beer, to play cards, or listen to the news on the radio.

The crisis for estiminets began in the 1970s. The advent of television and the general improvement in living conditions in homes, combined with the limitations of alcohol consumption for drivers, caused a drastic reduction in the number of places in the city.

The "Estaminet" was a family-run business. The owner, called "Baes" or "Boze" managed it directly with the help of his wife. Often, the wives played a very central role since many owners were the only nominal managers while in fact having another job.

Managing an estaminet required getting up at dawn to clean, light and warm the premise before the arrival of the first customers who started work shift at 6 a.m.

During the day, the atmosphere was quite calm except for public holidays or the days when celebrations were hosted. Estaminets gradually filled up after the end of the afternoon work shifts at the factories and reached the peak of attendance after the evening meal.

Estaminets were the "living room for people who didn't have a living room in their house".

The owner (or "patron" in French) would interact with customers for whom he was a point of reference and a source of information.

The most delicate moment of the day was closing time, when it was necessary to gently persuad the most recalcitrant customers to make their way home.

Some estaminets also served food and had waitresses, mainly country girls who worked hard for little money and often suffered customer harassment.

Food stalls selling street food could often be found outside the more popular estaminets.

Estaminets also became gathering places for sports enthusiasts and fans of the teams and meeting places of various associations and clubs.

Cafes were mostly owned by breweries (brasserie). There was a clear hierarchy in the work organisation; the Director was in charge of staff management and administration. At the counter there was a waiter in charge of collecting orders under the close supervision of a "hotesse".

Then there were the other waiters, led by the maitre, who took orders from the customers and served them. The waiters were equipped with service clothing (usually a black and white holding) and were trained to be polite, affable and smiling.

La "Cagnotte"

In the 19th century and until the beginning of the twentieth century, several estaminets also provided "savings accounts". There were wooden crates with the name of the customer, or the association managing the savings. Every month, on a given day and time, the worker had to pay his share. The owner of the building also served as a banker.

This system had positive aspects (workers were obliged to save money and there were penalties in cases of non-payment), but it also generated abuse (indiscriminate enrichment of the owner of the premises or exorbitant interest rates on loans granted).

The Games

Cafes and estaminets were the favourite places for games as well. Chess, checkers, cards, billiards, dice games (the Pietjesbak also called 421 or the Vogelpik) or the Schuiftafel (a sand board on which players throw tin tokens with the help of a stick).

Today, it is still possible to play board games in several estaminets and Brussels bars.

In the estaminets with a garden, there were popular games such as bowls, shooting games, and a typically Brussels game, the Mijole.

Undoubtedly, there were also illicit games related to betting.

Brussels Today

Today, Brussels is experiencing a real "Beer Renaissance" or "Beer Revolution". A phenomenon that the COVID pandemic crisis only partially slowed down.

The renaissance, or revolution, began in 2010 when Brasserie de la Senne made its appearance in a Brussels that seemed destined to be ruled by industrial breweries.

Then others came: En Stomelings, Ermitage, Brussels Beer Project...until today when we have nineteen breweries on the territory of the Brussels Capital Region.

The number is set to increase in the short term as there are several projects ready to launch themselves in the field. If we also count the Beer Firms and Gypsy Brewers, the numbers are even greater.

The dark age of beer in Brussels, when only Cantillon existed is just a bad memory. The craft beer revolution has arrived in the capital of the beer kingdom, Belgium.

The new breweries that have appeared in recent years, however, have little or nothing to do with the Belgian tradition.

Following the new wave that started in the USA, exploded in the UK and that now is well underway in almost all of Europe, even Brussels (and Ghent and to a lesser extent Antwerp) has seen new innovative breweries flourish, revisiting the great classics and focusing on styles previously uncommon in these lands.

We move from the classic British styles of Brasserie de la Jungle to the German styles (yes, German beers...in

Belgium) of Brasserie de la Mule to the reinterpretation of classic Belgian styles of l'Ermitage, l'Annexe and En Stomelings.

In addition to this, many Brewpubs have opened recently.

COVID and rising energy and raw material prices have made it difficult to attempt to emulate large breweries.

Today in Brussels, excluding the historic Brasserie Cantillon, Brasserie de la Senne and Brussels Beer Project are the only two breweries that produce large volumes of beer and export a fair amount of beer. Those who have tried to imitate them are experiencing difficulties and now the winning models are the brewpubs that give higher margins and create a direct link with customers.

The first example was La Source, a brewpub that after a slow start became a model for many others.

More generally, even in Brussels, in the last 5 years, the wind of returning to craftsmanship has begun to blow. This provides an alternative vision to the industrial logic aimed at enhancing small-scale production, the quality of products and the link with the local community.

This process has led, in many cities in Western Europe, to revitalisation of disused, neglected and derelict areas, previously occupied by industrial buildings.

This is also the case in Brussels. Most of the new breweries have arisen along the canal that divides the municipality of Molenbeek from the city centre, in the Tour&Taxis district and in the municipalities of Saint Gilles, Anderlecht and Schaerbeek; all areas characterised by a great industrial past.

The concentration of breweries in the neighbourhood of Tour&Taxis is particularly interesting. Previously there were only old buildings and a high level of dereliction. The area is now destined to become the "Beer Mile"[2] of Brussels. Within a few meters of each other, you can find En Stomelings and Source. A few hundred meters away, there is the Brasserie de la Senne. And if you cross the Kanaal, you find Brasserie Oskare.

Another interesting aspect is that the new breweries are being built along the Kanaal. It is reminiscent of the past of the city, where many breweries operated along the banks of the river Senne.

The peculiarity of almost all the new breweries is the fact that they were opened by renovating abandoned sheds or railway premises, in areas where before it was not advisable to go.

The policy of incentives put in place by the Brussels-Capital Region (grants, low-interest loans, provision of spaces under favourable conditions[3]) is certainly encouraging this process.

Brewing is an engine of development and recovery of previously marginalised areas of the city. A kind of "beer gentrification". This is it what it means to invest in brewing today in Brussels.

In the next chapters, we will look at the nineteen craft breweries in Brussels. I interviewed the brewers to better

---

[2] The Bermondsey Beer Mile is a challenge worthy of any self-respecting beer fiend, stretching a whopping 1.4 miles through the streets and railway arches of South London.

[3] Greenbizz sustainable economy SME park; Brusoc micro-credit.

understand their approaches and to listen to their vision of the future of beer in Brussels.

Cantillon

Rue Gheude 56, 1070 Anderlecht

Visiting Brasserie Cantillon at Rue Gheude 56 in Anderlecht, a 5-minute walk from the Gare du Midi, is a must for every beer enthusiast. Despite its worldwide fame, it is still a traditional family brewery.

In order to find the origins of the brewery, we need to go back to 1894 when Auguste Cantillon, a cereal producer, bought a brewery for his children in Hondzocht, a district of the municipality of Lembeek in the Pajotteland area.

Paul Cantillon, had married Marie De Troch, daughter of a famous brewer, and after a few years of experience decided to abandon the family business and open a new one in Brussels. In the 1890, Paul and Marie opened their Lambic blendery in Anderlecht.

They chose Anderlecht for its proximity to Brussels-Midi train station and waterways.

They bought Lambic from their relatives who still worked in Lembeek and fermented it in their barrels in Brussels, producing Gueuze, Faro, Kriek and Mars.

In 1937 Paul Cantillon, along with his sons Marcel and Robert, bought a plant for the production of Lambic; it was the official birth of Brasserie Cantillon.

Brasserie Cantillon survived World War II but then received an almost fatal blow with the advent of the lager beers. The consumption collapse of Gueze brought Cantillon to the brink of failure in 1968.

The elder brother, Robert, nearing his retirement and without heirs, sold the shares to his brother Marcel whose only daughter, Claude, had married Jean-Pierre Van Roy in 1967 who had helped his father-in-law in the Brasserie since 1963.

In 1970 Jean-Pierre, who at the time worked for Philips Company and was a teacher, decided to dedicate himself full-time to the brewery soon becoming the real manager.

In 1978 he inaugurated the Gueuze Museum, which has become one of the most visited attractions in Brussels.

Jean-Pierre, unlike many other brewers, decided not to use any sweeteners to produce Lambic, becoming the most ardent defender of the traditional method. Forced to acquire the shares of the other members of the Cantillon family, Jean Pierre and the brewery accumulated huge debts, which only in 1993 was repaid by hard work and enormous sacrifices.

Unlike the other producers of Lambic and Gueuze, Cantillon does not carry the name "Oude" on the label because according to Jean-Pierre there is only traditional Lambic, the rest is a different thing. The brasserie refused to join the Horal (High Council for Traditional Lambic Beers) cartel due to the presence of industrial producers.

The battle against the industrialisation of Lambic was a constant in Jean Pierre's life, so the motto "Le temps ne respecte pas ce qui se fait sans lui" (time does not respect what is done without him).

In 1989, Jean, the son of Jean-Pierre and his wife Claude, joined the team. Like his father many years before, Jean learned the new job "on the field" in his daily work at the brewery.

He brought some innovations such as the use of new barrels (previously they had used barrels belonging to the De Troch Brewery) and the use of the crown cap coupled with the cork cap, to avoid carbon dioxide leakage.

Today Cantillon is known all over the world and its beers are famous and sought after by enthusiasts.

The main beers produced are:

- Gueuze 100 % Lambic
- Kriek 100 % Lambic with cherries
- Rosé de Gambrinus (Raspberry-flavoured Lambic)
- Grand Cru Bruocsella (Lambic, unmixed)
- Iris (seasonal beer without wheat use, so technically not a Lambic)
- Vigneronne (Lambic with Italian white grapes)
- Saint-Lamvinus (with merlot and cabernet-franc grapes from farms in the Libourne area, France)
- Foù Foune (Lambic with apricot)
- Lou Pepe Gueuze
- Lou Pepe Kriek
- Lou Pepe Framboise (Raspberry)
- Mamouche (Blend of Lambic and elderflowers)
- Cuvee Saint Gilloise (Blend of Lambic with use of Hallertau hops, dedicated to the football team of Union St. Gilloise)
- Nath (Blend by Lambic and rhubarb)

There are also other limited-edition beers, such as Druiven Lambic, which have become collectible pieces. They are usually sold online at a certain time of a certain day, produced for beer cafes around the world or sold at the brewery at certain times of the year.

Unfortunately, there is a flourishing black market (as with 3 Fonteinen, another "holy monster" of the Gueuze) with bottles resold in dizzying figures by opportunists and unscrupulous businessmen. Brasserie Cantillon fights this phenomenon by recording the data of the customer who buys the most highly rated products.

Whatever you look at it, Brasserie Cantillon represents the history of beer and consequently part of the history of Brussels.

That is why I wished to interview Jean Pierre Van Roy (and it was a great honour to be able to do it).

He and his wife, Claude, handed over management of the brewery to their talented son Jean in 2009. But very often on Saturdays they go to the brewery to serve Gueuze and Lambic to visitors and entertain them with their stories.

After agreeing with his son Jean to interview his father, I went to Brasserie Cantillon. It was a Saturday and outside there was a long line of customers waiting to buy the Sang Bleu (formerly known as Camerise), a Lambic blended with Haskap berries.

Madame Claude (who also speaks a little Italian) came to pick up me outside the brewery and took me to her husband in the studio just behind the counter.

There I experienced one of the most beautiful and interesting beer-related discussion that I have ever had.

Interview with Jean Pierre Van Roy:

Dear Jean Pierre, what is your first memory of the Brasserie Cantillon?

My first memory is the discovery of the Brasserie itself. I met my wife Claude in 1962, I didn't know she was a brewer's daughter, and I didn't know of the Gueuze Cantillon. I only knew Mort Subite.

In 1964, I was invited to spend Christmas Eve at Claude's house. There, were also her parents Marcelle and Jean and the brasserie accountant with his wife.

We ate and drank well. When we finished, it was 1 or maybe 2 o'clock at night, I looked out the window and saw it was snowing. There were at least 25 centimetres of snow. At the time, I had a Lambretta scooter and I lived in Woluwe Saint-Pierre. It was unthinkable to try to go back home.

Marcelle Cantillon, my future father-in-law, told me to park the Lambretta in the Brasserie and gave me the keys. At the time, they lived just 300 meters from the Brasserie. I opened the door and walked in for the first time. I have a strong memory especially about the smell. It made an extraordinary impression on me even though it was totally dark. I couldn't see anything as I didn't know where the light was.

The first job was to learn how to make beer. It started at 4:30 in the morning, the working day was long, we did not have the same boiler as today and needed time to prepare hot water, about 4 hours to prepare the wort.

My first working memory is when I was around the vat with a thermometer and listened to all that my father-in-law told me to do. He taught me everything.

Lambic was close to the extinction. When did you perceive that something was changing?

In the 1960s, business was very bad. To sell beers it was necessary to visit several cafes, to offer a tasting and hope that they would order it. Not many cafes owners ordered beers like Gueuze. One day, I was at Claude's home. At the time, we were engaged. Her father Marcelle entered, he had just returned from one of these tours with poor results, he sat in the dining room and started crying.

This was the brewer's life. It was a time when the brewer had to offer drinks to live and drink with the potential customer to sell. The occupational disease of brewers was liver cirrhosis, my father-in-law Marcelle died of that as many others.

I started my job doing the same thing. I was doing these tours with my father-in-law.

One day in the early 1970s, George Michiels, President of the Rue Haute Trader Association in the Marolles district, entered my office. He told me that we were the only ones in Brussels who made a real traditional Gueuze and that he wanted support to relaunch the Rue Haute parade. It was a street parade, very colourful with majorettes, fanfare etc. He wanted us to serve Lambic and Faro directly from our barrels.

My father-in-law said that I was crazy, that no one was selling beer on the street. I decided to do that. I stood with the barrels in front of the Michiels tailors' shop (which closed in 2010) and I had a great success, both from a public and financial point of view.

In fact, I had the opportunity to sell my beers to a different market than the one who usually went to cafes. Many curious people stopped to ask questions about Lambic, Faro and Gueuze.

In January or February of the following year, a journalist from "La Libre Belgique" called me. He told me that in October he had been at the Rue Haute parade and had tasted our beers and asked me for a meeting to write an article about us.

My father-in-law was doubtful, the brasserie at the time was not a welcoming environment. Instead, I thought that the authenticity of the environment could be seductive. The journalist was enthusiastic about the visit. However, to have the article published, we needed to buy an advertising space in the newspaper.

He produced a beautiful article that I will put in my Conservatory of Lambic.

When the article was published, Marcelle was in Houyet in the Ardennes where he owned a house. He was woken up at 7 a.m. by enthusiastic neighbours who told him he had ended up in the newspaper.

Two days later a lady who had read the article called me and asked to visit the brewery. We then hosted the visit of a first group and others followed later.

In 1974, a painter asked me to organise a vernissage at the brasserie and that day there were 300 people. I did six guided tours, all alone.

In 1975, I participated in an exhibition organised by the Province of Brabant on the breweries and estaminets of the province.

In 1976, Pierre Bruylandt, a journalist of the newspaper Le Vlan, a free newspaper that arrived in all the mailboxes, wrote a long article about the brasserie. I told him I wanted to make it a living museum.

In 1978, I created an ASBL, the Musée Bruxellois de la Gueuze, a cultural enterprise that was independent of the brasserie, which was a commercial enterprise. It was the turning point. A new audience began to arrive, initially people from Brussels, then Belgian, then European and finally from all over the world. In 1979, we reached 3000 visitors. In 2015, we exceeded 50000 and last May 7, 2022 we reached the millionth visitor.

Thanks to the museum, Brasserie Cantillon has avoided extinction.

Meanwhile my wife's family did not want to continue with the business. There were three sons in the Cantillon family who could have continued with the business but none of them wished to.

It was the end of the 1960s and business was very bad. At the time, I was working with records and music and I was a teacher, I offered to continue the business and they told me that I was crazy.

When they saw that things were getting better, they decided to leave the company. They had the right to do so, but they asked for an astronomical figure. There was a huge difference between my assessment and theirs. They came out of the business in 1978. I was doing well before, but because of their exit, I was hugely indebted and managed to settle all my debts only in 1993.

I was working with outdated materials, if there was a food control agency, they would have shut me down. I couldn't do anything else. We wouldn't be here today.

A turning point was 1988. In the 1980s, I had Japanese and American visitors. The brewers of Kirin and Sapporo breweries came to visit the brasserie and I have been exporting to Japan since 1989.

In the early 1990s, Americans began to take an interest in my products.

I stopped brewing in 2006. I received a beautiful letter from a banker who was retiring and told me that he would never believe Cantillon would do it. I spent years knocking on the banks' doors to convince them to grant me more credit to be able to pay staff and suppliers, securing with obligations, so doing more debt. I got a cash debit of 2 million Belgian francs.

In 1993, I repaid all the debts and brasserie became mine. I owned already the 25% of it, the part that Marcelle had left us. We worked and fought so much for it.

In Italy, we know Brasserie Cantillon thanks to Lorenzo Dabove, Kuaska, when did you meet him? And when did the relationship between Cantillon and Italy begin?

I have known him well since the late '90s. He came here for the first time in 1982 to visit the Museum of Gueuze. Lorenzo fell in love with this beer. I regularly write letters to the 500 members of the Gueuze Museum. I write it in French and Lorenzo translates them into Italian. The other versions are in Flemish and English. Lorenzo also leads the tour visits to the brewery during the "Brassin public".

In 1979, an Italian magazine, the "Civiltà del Bere", wrote an excellent report about the brasserie.

We started working with some Italian importers in the late 1980s.

In recent years, Cantillon organised unique events such as Quintessence and Zwanze Day. What is the idea behind them?

Quintessence was my idea. The first was organised in 1998 to celebrate the 20th anniversary of the Gueuze Museum. I decided to organise an event with the aim of checking our products every two years. It was an event organised by the ASBL of the Museum of Gueuze in which besides the Cantillon beers, we offered other local products for tasting also. It was open to up to 500 people for space reasons. I once organised one for a bank that asked me as an event for their employees.

Then there was a further development. My son took over this activity and decided to involve other breweries as well. It's become a different thing.

The Zwanze is an idea of my son, an original idea, but that goes beyond Lambic. It generates great publicity because every year the Zwanze is released simultaneously in clubs around the world.

I also do the "Zwanze", but of another type of Zwanze. In Brussels dialect, the term "Zwanze" means joke. And I make a lot of jokes. I like to do it.

Once I made a joke to the members of the museum announcing that I was macerating a plant, Saponaria Officinalis, which in the past was used to wash since it is a natural detergent, with my Lambic.

I called it Zypsoplambic and I had also asked cartoonist Louis-Michel Carpentier to prepare a label that I sent to all the members of the museum. Many of them believed it and I was overwhelmed by orders.

In recent years, Druiven Lambic is very fashionable among beer enthusiasts. Cantillon produces different ones, when and how are they brewed?

Druiven Lambic are traditional beers. They already existed at the beginning of the 20th century. There were grapes in the south of Brussels. In 1973, I made my first Druiven Lambic with Belgian grapes.

I made one for Pascal Delbeck, winemaker of the Bordeaux Region. It was the first Lambic mixed with Bordeaux grapes and I called it Saint Lamvinus. "Lam" for Lambic and "Vinus" for wine. I took part in Vinexpo in Bordeaux and organised tastings in his castle.

Today, we have many and different ones. Many people are looking for them. I don't like them much, I prefer traditional products, but I understand that the world has changed.

Tell me about the project of the Conservatory of Lambic and Gueuze

This is my last big project. Over the years, I collected a lot of historical documentation that I want to preserve and leave as a legacy. This project is a dream for me. I spoke about it for the first time in 2005 to a Flemish journalist who had asked me about my plans for the future.

The work began on 9 May 2022 and will end in early October, and then when everything is ready, we will organise an inauguration.

Right now, the Brasserie has no roof and Lambic's barrels look up at the sky. It's nothing new to me, it was so in 1984.

How do you think the Brussels beer scene will evolve in the coming years? How do you see the future of Lambic?

The future of breweries will depend about consumers. For an entire generation, Gueuze wasn't appreciated at all. The generation born after the war has experienced the success of Coca-Cola and the development of the food industry that has led to a general change of taste. The arrival of supermarkets has brought about a new form of trade and has led to a standardisation of products. They have marketed products with an "easy" taste. This led to the death of the sour beers.

Many of my colleagues started to add sugar to please their customers.

My father-in-law, Marcelle, once told me of an episode he had witnessed, in which a representative of Belle-Vue, while in a cafe, rolled a bottle on the floor and asked the holder to open it and serve it, ensuring that it would be as clear as a crystal.

Traditional brewers were forced to change in order to survive, the alternative was to close.

I don't know how the situation will evolve, the public has become complacent and does not react, beer now costs too much. Even Lambic costs too much although production costs are not high. Here, it's still reasonable.

We need to plan for the future and make the right choices. An excellent Brasserie that produced Gueuze, the Brasserie De Neve in Schepdaal, of which I knew the family well, disappeared because there was no agreement between the heirs.

We have 3 children and 7 grandchildren; we will assess in one or two years as to how to move forward. Together with the construction of the Conservatoire del Lambic this is my main concern.

What's your favourite beer from Cantillon?

Without any doubt the Lambic and the Gueuze. They are exceptional and incredible beers. They make themselves; the brewer is the slave of his own Lambic and his Gueuze. This beer is made by itself, during the night, while the brewer sleeps. The brewer just needs to be careful and respect what they taught him. All other products, Kriek, Framboise and Druiven Lambic are manipulated.

I drink a little of beers and only good products, I have an excellent wine cave, but I consider Lambic and Gueuze the best products to drink.

Brasserie de la Senne

Drève Anna Boch 19/21, 1000 Brussels

If the Cantillon brewery brews the historic beer in Brussels, the Brassserie de la Senne is undoubtedly the one which has started and led the revolution of craft breweries in the city. It is one of the best-known brands, in Belgium and abroad, of the new generation of producers.

The name chosen by Bernard Leboucq and Yvan De Baets, the two brewers and founders, is a tribute to the Senne, the river that crosses Brussels and is linked with the brewing history of this corner of the world.

The Brasserie de la Senne is a perfect combination of tradition and innovation; traditional Belgian styles updated with a constant, but limited use of hops.

The brewery first appeared in 2003 in Sint-Pieters-Leeuw in Flemish Brabant under the name St Peter's Brouwerij. In 2005, the Brasserie de la Senne came into being. It remained without a fixed location until December 2010 when it opened a site in the municipality of Molenbeek in the building that previously housed an industrial bakery. The brewery has been in its current location since December 2019 with the inauguration of the new site of 4500 square meters in the Tour&Taxis area with a tap room (the Zenne Bar, open Tuesday to Friday from 16 to 20 and Saturday from 12 to 8 pm) in an area that is becoming the Belgian Beer Mile.

Brasserie de la Senne has made a long journey thanks to extraordinary beers such as the Taras Boulba (a very drinkable Belgian Ale), the iconic Zinnebir, and the Jambe de Bois (one of the most "dangerous" Triple for drinkability on the market).

The brewery produces another dozen beers, several of which are "seasonal" and dedicated to particular events of the city.

To better understand the future of beer in Brussels, I had to discuss it with someone who built the foundations of the rebirth of craft beer in the city; Yvan De Baets.

Yvan, in addition to being a beer lover (and co-author of the latest Brussels beer guide, "Around Brussels in 80 Beers", written with Joe Stange in 2009) is a great lover and connoisseur of Brussels.

Chatting with him was really an immersion in the historical and cultural events of this incredible city.

Interview with Yvan De Baets:

Dear Yvan, how did the Brasserie de la Senne's adventure begin?

It all started 20 years ago. It was May 2002, I worked as a social worker with young people for the municipality of St.Josse. We were attending the Zinneke Parade[4]. At one point, when we were in front of the Belgacom Tower (now Proximus Tower) in the Gare du Nord area, I noticed a boy pushing a trolley full of beers. It was

---

[4] The Zinneke Parade is a biennial parade held in the City of Brussels, Belgium, since 2000. It is a cultural event organised by the Zinneke Association, which brings together at each edition about 1500 participants. A different theme is chosen for each parade.
The parade was established with the aim of connecting the many different cultures, communities and districts within Brussels.

Bernard, my current business partner. Between one beer and the other, he told me that he had opened a squat in Ixelles and that the organisers of the Zinneke Parade had asked him to create a beer for the event. He then produced what was the first version of Zinnebir. We exchanged phone numbers to stay in touch.

For a year, nothing happened except that Bernard tried unsuccessfully to open a small brewery in Ixelles. I decided to support him but unfortunately the municipality of Ixelles, after raising our expectations, in the end did not support us.

Bernard found a small building in Sint-Pieters-Leeuw in the suburbs of Brussels. It was an old warehouse of the Gueuzerie Stokerij Moriau. We rented it at a low rent and bought second-hand material for a total capacity of 400 litres. He decided to call it St Peter's Brouwerij and that was actually our first brewery.

It was 2003 and, in the meantime, I had decided to definitely change my life and follow my passion; brewing.

I had studied Political Science and worked for five years as a social worker. I had been brewing at home since 1997, I read many books, visited many breweries, worked as a volunteer in different breweries and obviously tasted many beers.

I decided to take a brewing course at the Meurice Institute in Anderlecht. Bernard already had a brewing training; my role was as technical consultant.

In 2004, I started working part time at the Brewery De Ranke for two days a week. They were friends of mine; I knew them very well. The rest of the week, I worked at our brewery.

At the end of 2005, we were forced to leave the brewery in Sint-Pieters-Leeuw because it had become too small. So, we decided to formally join forces and create the Brasserie de la Senne, seeking a location in Brussels where we had always wanted to open a brewery.

The reference to "Senne", the river thanks to which Brussels exists, is due to the fact that we are both from Brussels and we love this crazy city. Many historic breweries in Brussels were located along the river and even our first brewery in Sint-Pieters-Leeuw was not far away.

The Senne is the only river that flows through all regions of Belgium. It rises in Wallonia, flows through Brussels and ends in Flanders. It is a symbol that unites Belgium; and so, for us it has a lot of meaning.

Funding was a big problem. At the time, banks did not grant loans easily for such projects. Today it's much easier.

The banks told us we were two crazies! It took us 5 years to raise the money and to find a location in the municipality of Molenbeek.

In the meantime, we brewed our beers at the De Ranke brewery as they had extra capacity. I should point out that we rented their facilities, and that the entire production process was under our supervision. Having worked with them I knew them very well. When I started it was the first year they produced at the brewery, before that they had brewed at the Deca Brouwerij.

At some point we wanted to launch a new beer, the Jambe de Bois. But as De Ranke had no capacity, we went to other friends, the Brasserie Thiriez, in northern France, an excellent craft brewery located between Lille and Dunkerque. Every two months I went there to brew beer.

Finally, in December 2010, we brewed the first batch beer brewed entirely, 100%, in Brussels.

December is a very important month for us. We started in December 2003 in Sint-Pieters-Leeuw, left Sint-Pieters-Leeuw in December 2005, started in Molenbeek in December 2010 and started at the current location in December 2019.

We stayed at the Molenbeek site for seven years, until it became too small. It took two years to build the current site, but in the meantime, we continued to brew beer in Molenbeek without any production stop. Now we use the old brewery as a storage room and to allow some beers to age in barrels.

Why did you choose this area? Other breweries have also done so, do you think a "Belgian Beer Mile" is developing?

No. In the US it would work, but here no. In Brussels, it is not a given that if in one area there are more breweries, that more people come to visit them. The city is not big enough. Moreover, I do not believe in the added value of the concentration of activities of the same type.

However, I believe very much in the development of this area that is experiencing a sudden growth with a residential plan that anticipates the creation of a thousand apartments and then offices and the project of the Gare Maritime.

In a direct line, we are 2 kilometres far from the Grand Place. In this area, a new heart of the city is developing.

Brasserie de la Senne was the first brewery to open in Brussels after many years. Before, there was only Cantillon. When did you realise that "you had made it" and that you had contributed to the launching of a revolution, the craft beer revolution in Brussels?

We understood this when we saw that other craft breweries opening in Brussels; in fact, we opened the way for them. We helped many to launch their projects, we were the first to prove that it was possible.

When we started it was really hard, it was hard to find a location, and it was even harder to get loans.

Today it is much easier because banks have seen that it is economically viable to open a brewery. However, they have not understood that the market is now saturated and that it will not be easy in the coming years.

Brussels is the capital of Belgium, there are many bars, all the breweries in Belgium aspire to sell their products here.

Aren't you optimistic about the future of the beer scene in Brussels?

This is an economic reality. The market cannot grow indefinitely. The same thing happened in the United States. At some point, you have to stop. It is a fact that while many want to try, the cake is limited, and it will not expand. I can't tell you when, if in 2 in 5 or even in 10 years. But the logic points to that.

I think there could be room for very small projects where everything is sold on site, such as Mazette, for example, self-sustainable projects.

But if you want to reach a certain size, the competition is now ruthless. Many people think this is some kind of hippie world, I'd love think so, but that's not the case. It's a complicated world.

Today I would never start a project like the one we started twenty years ago. We are where we are because we started a long time ago.

As far as we are concerned, we do not want to grow without limit. At some point, we will stop because we want to maintain a human dimension that allows direct control over quality. If you get too big there is a risk of losing the soul of the project.

I understand that it's easy to say and maybe hard to believe but I still make beer out of passion, I'm passionate about my job, maybe even more than before. I make beer at least once a week, I don't want to be just a manager, even if I have to do that too.

Tell me about Zinnebir, your most iconic beer. It is a beer that has become a symbol for Brussels. Personally, the first time I saw it, I was impressed by the words "Brussels people ale". Someone also talks about a new style launched with the Zinnebir...Brussels pale ale.

You're right. In 2005, we changed the label and immediately put this phrase "Brussels People Ale". To have it become the beer of Brussels people was a dream at the time, and honestly we didn't think it would come true. Now it has become so.

It is a beer of character, with a balance between malts and hops that represents our style. With this beer we have reached a circle of people that goes well beyond fans and connoisseurs. What I call "normal people."

Our biggest win was being able to get our beers out of the craft beer bars (where we still are) and reach the corner bars where normal people go. When I see my beers being drank in one of these bars, I still get excited. That's great.

You mentioned your cask ageing project at the Molenbeek site. Are you planning to produce your Lambic in the future? Others are doing it in Brussels.

I have great respect and admiration for Cantillon. I forgot to tell you that I worked there for two years for two days a week as a guide to the museum. I needed money as every penny we made at Brasserie de la Senne was reinvested into the project.

I love spontaneous fermentation, I love Lambic. But we're never going to be a brewery like that. Yes, we will do some experiments, but on a small scale, not with large volumes.

Do you think participating in a beer festival is an added value?

I don't believe much in the instrument itself. From a commercial point of view, the gain is zero. They are interesting for beer enthusiasts, less so for brewers. Also participating in a beer festival means a lot more work for the team, especially during the weekend.

What's your favourite beer from Brasserie de la Senne?

I have two. The first is the Taras Boulba, my heart beer, light but with character. The second is Zenne Pils. In our range, they are the two most difficult beers to make.

In general, low fermentation beers are the most difficult for a brewer. You have to be perfect. When you produce a good pils, it means that you probably produce other styles in an excellent way.

Producing a pils pushes you to higher levels, it pushes you to become a better brewer. It also obliges you to be humble because with the slightest distraction you make mistakes.

Brewing is never boring, there are so many things that are not intuitive, that you do not understand immediately and therefore require additional reflection. It's easy to get nervous but impossible to get bored.

What about your favourite beer from another Brussels brewery?

The Lambic and the Gueuze of Cantillon.

En Stoemelings

Rue Dieudonné Lefèvre 37, 1020 Brussels

En Stomelings[5] was the third brewery opened in Brussels. It is a brewery with a strong imprint of Brussels; the name, the motto and the name of the beers.

The brewery always characterises itself by producing classic Belgian styles such as Tripel or Saison in the picturesque Marolles district. The beginning was very "basic" with beers bottled in 0.75 bottles with a label hanging from the cap. Today, it is a classic product and is evolving towards spontaneous fermentations due to strong collaboration with Cantillon.

En Stomeling is located in Tour&Taxis area and, along with the No Science brewery, is one of the frontrunners of what is becoming the "Belgian Beer Mile".

It is open every day but lacks a real tap room (although tables are often placed outside where you can taste the beers). The visits are on Saturday afternoon.

I spoke to Alexis, one of the heads of the team, about En Stomelings and the future of beer in Brussels.

Interview with Alexis Boisseau[6]:

---

[5] In July 2024, En Stomelings handed over equipment to 'Amère à boire' cafés. Their beers will be produced always in Brussels by a sub-contractor.
[6] In 2023, Alexis launched is own project Osma BXL, a barrel aged beer project.

How did the adventure of En Stomelings begin?

The brewery was created in 2013 by Denys Van Elewyck and Samuel Languy. They have been friends since they were 12 years old. Denys was an archaeology student who brewed at home, Samuel had just returned from India where he was a video game developer.

Together, they worked on a prototype beer, the Curieuse Neus, a Triple that has become the symbol of En Stomelings.

The brewery was officially opened in October 2014, in 2015 they found their first location, a small place of 100 square meters in the historic district of Marolles.

I arrived at that point, I did a two-year internship and then I joined the team. At the time we made beer in 200 litre pots. We worked a lot with local projects like Recyclart and made beers in dark 0.75 bottles of champagne. Sometimes, we sold kegs to the Moeder Lambic. At the time, the Brussels beer scene was very quiet and we wanted to try to offer an alternative to large-scale industrial beer.

To grow and operate our project, however, we needed a larger location, so we moved here in Greenbizz, in Tour&Taxis area. Here, we have reached a production of 18 hectolitres.

What styles of beer do you focus on?

Our basic range is based on classic, Belgian and non-Belgian styles. We recently launched the "Xp Sauvage" range in which we blend our classic beers (such as Curieuse Neus or Tanteke) with Lambic from Cantillon, with cider, with wine or let them age in cask.

We brew, together with Cantillon, the 1897, which is the official beer of the football team of the Union St. Gilloise. It is a blend between a Saison and the young Lambic (1 year) from Cantillon.

We experiment with a 20-litre tank to test the beers in a controlled environment like the brewery.

What does it mean "En Stomelings"?

En Stomelings in Brussels dialect means "secret" or "under cover". Denys and Samuel sold their first beers without licence. The newspaper "La Derniere Heure" published an article announcing the birth of the third Brussels brewery. They then immediately contacted the customs office who gave them a month to comply with all the legal formalities. Hence the name. It is a nice expression that foreigners do not know but find nice.

What about your motto "Het is ça va"?

It's a mix of French and Flemish that literally means "everything is fine". It represents our philosophy, an attitude of goodness and inclusion that has always distinguished us.

We have a small team without pyramid structures that aims to make great beers.

Other breweries have also settled in this area, do you think is it the beginning of a "Belgian Beer Mile"?

Brussels is the capital of beer. Visibility for a brewery is important. If you create an area where so many breweries are concentrated in, it is only a positive thing because it attracts beer tourism. We also produce different beers so there is a positive competition. By the way Mathieu (the brewer of La Source) studied with me and it's nice to find him here, just few meters away.

How do you think the Brussels beer scene will evolve in the coming years?

The market is saturated. I don't see much space.

There are many interesting new projects. At this point in in time, it is necessary to brew and sell directly on site. Nowadays, it is too complicated to develop another model because it is difficult to work with large volumes.

Certainly, with a brewpub you need to create a calendar of events to attract people; but this also has a positive effect on the neighbourhood because it brings more life. Many breweries are located in neighbourhoods that previously were simply forgotten by the community.

At the level of the Brussels breweries, there was an attempt to put all together in an association. But it is complicated, there are different ideas and philosophies. Maybe, we will try again in the future.

What's your favourite beer from En Stomelings?

Tanteke, a saison. It is a style that I love a lot and on which I work a lot. A lot of barrel beers we're working on are based on saison. It is a historical style of Belgium, a solid and refreshing beer.

What is your favourite beer from another Brussels brewery?

Taras Boulba. Because it is a beer of extraordinary drinkability and because Brasserie de la Senne has opened the doors to all of us. In Belgium I also love De Ranke's beers.

Brussels Beer Project

Quai de Biestebroeck 23, 1070 Anderlecht — BBP South

Rue Antoine Dansaert 188, 1000 Brussels — Dansaert Brewery

Rue du Bailli 1/A, 1000 Brussels — BBP Bailli

The Brussels Beer Project is one of the most discussed and successful beer projects on the Brussels beer scene.

It was established in 2013 by Olivier de Brauwere and Sébastien Morvan and in less than ten years they have become a big player on the scene. Their motto provides a crystal and clear view of their philosophy: "Leave the Abbey, Join the playground".

They experiment (almost every week) with many different ingredients and techniques.

The icing on the cake was the launch of their first Lambic (the first produced in Brussels in 50 years, after Cantillon) with a spectacular, and marketing oriented, public brewing at Grand Place in December 2021.

BBP currently has three sites; the brewery located in the municipality of Anderlecht in Port-South, the Bailli tap room (opened what was the well-known Irish Pub, Michael Collins) and the historic Dansaert site now destined for the Lambic project and spontaneous fermentations.

The Brussels Beer Project is both loved and criticised by many. For some, it is the "Brewdog" of Belgium. To understand more about it, I had a chat with Sébastien Morvan, one of the two founders.

Interview with Sébastien Morvan:

How did the Brussels Beer Project's adventure begin?

I met with my partner, Olivier, at College in Canada. We were both passionate about beer and we tasted a lot of beer together. For our 30th birthday, we wanted to do something special and something related to beer seemed to us the most interesting thing.

We started brewing beer in 2012 with a 27-litre keg in Olivier's garage; we read books, watched videos on YouTube and read American homebrewers forums. We also had other friends who brewed. Opening a brewery seemed like a dream because we didn't have money, but we believed in the project and slowly it all became more serious. So, I decided to take a course at the Institute Meurice.

The Brussels Beer Project was officially launched in 2013. We found a location, the current Dansaert site. We bought all the equipment and obtained all the authorisations and finally we opened it in 2015.

Our first beer was the Delta IPA. It was chosen in a competition in 2013 between four prototypes (Alpha, Beta, Gamma and Delta).

You put Brussels in the name of your Brewery, how important is the connection with the city for you?

For us, the connection with Brussels is very important. I come from Brittany, a good part of the team is not Belgian, but we are all united by love for Brussels, we feel "Bruxellois". It's a fantastic, magical city. One of the most multicultural cities in the world.

I travelled a lot before moving here. In Brussels, I found a real home. One of our brewers, who worked as chief brewer in Jester King, told me that outside Texas he never found a place where he felt at home as in Brussels.

Brussels is a city that makes you feel at home. It is an honour for us to represent Brussels in Belgium and abroad with our beers in a new, fresh, innovative and creative way. It is also a city in transformation, and we are happy to contribute to the renewal of areas such as Anderlecht with our new enterprises.

Tell me about the philosophy of the Brussels Beer Project, your motto is "Leave the Abbey, join the playground". What does it mean?

Oliver and I travelled a lot. Belgian beers abroad are highly regarded. But these are centuries-old recipes. When we started, there were no novelties on the market. Belgium cannot leave the wave of new craft beers to Americans, English or Scandinavians. That's why we launch new recipes, we want to experiment and have fun. Traditional beers are too serious.

Our goal is to bring people closer to beer by breaking the pre-conceived patterns that have ruled in this world for so many years.

Your focus is on innovation, but you were also the first to produce a Lambic in Brussels after Cantillon, a

historic style for this city. What are you aiming to with this new project?

True. We launched our Lambic and soon we will have our Gueuze. Dansaert is the site we choose to develop this project. Few people know that many years ago there was a brewery there.

We know that we are dealing with something that has a crazy story but here too we want to subvert the rules. We want to experiment and try new techniques.

The model is the natural wines of Languedoc-Roussilon. We want to spread Lambic and Gueuze among people who like to drink beer, but who are not necessarily connoisseurs or beer geeks.

We have two fantastic brewers, Jordan Keeper, who worked for Jester King; and Tiago Falcone, a Brazilian, who has worked in many breweries in Europe. He is a specialist in Barrel-Aging. They know that they can play with the rules and experiment. We also collaborate with projects such as PermaFungi, a champion of the circular economy, and with different fruit producers. We don't want to replicate the story but create something different.

Are you planning new openings in Brussels?

We plan to open new tap rooms in Brussels.

In recent years have you opened tap rooms abroad, in Paris, France, and Tokyo in Japan, are you planning new openings?

For now, it is not our priority to expand into other countries. We have a good market abroad but now the priority is to consolidate at the regional level.

You organise a successful beer festival every year, the Wanderlust, tell me about it.

It is an annual beer festival. In the last two editions, we organised it at Place Saint Catherine. It's a way to celebrate with our community. I have lived in 8 countries; I love to travel and share. The festival is dedicated to those who love to travel and share. We invite breweries that we like from all over the world, and people we love to be with.

Competition in the world of craft beers is an abstract concept. There is a lot to learn or share with other breweries. It's a festival where beer isn't the only focus.

How do you think the Brussels beer scene will evolve in the coming years?

I think there is room for more breweries, in Brussels, but especially in Belgium. Not necessarily large breweries, but also small enterprises. We need it to maintain our status as a brewing country and to demonstrate that we know how to innovate while maintaining a high level of quality. We have quality, but we need courage.

What is your favourite beer from the Brussels Beer Project?

It would be easy to tell you that it's next one, you're always excited when you make a new beer. I drink a lot of Juice Junkie (NEIPA) but Delta IPA, our first beer, is the one I'm most tied to.

What is your favourite beer from another Brussels brewery?

I like several beers from La Source and l'Ermitage.

L'Ermitage Nanobrasserie

Rue Lambert Crickx 26, 1070 Anderlecht

This beautiful urban beer project was born from the passion of three friends: Henry Bensaria, François Simon and Nacim Menu, who in 2013 began to brew at home in their apartment at rue de l'Ermitage in the municipality of Ixelles.

In 2016, they decided to turn their passion into a profession and create, in the premises of Brasserie de Bastogne, their first beer; The Lantern, a Pale Ale.

In 2017, they opened their production site in Anderlecht, a few meters away from Cantillon. The production site includes a tap room. The success with the public led them to open a bar, in St. Gilles, and a shop where they sell also their natural wines.

They produce a wide range of beers, focusing on British and new wave beer styles. Recently, they are working on spontaneous fermentation and barrel-aged beers.

I met Nacim at the SWAFF Beer festival and we agreed to see each other at the brewery, where in front of a couple of fresh beers, he told me about their adventure.

Interview with Nacim Menu:

How and when did your adventure begin?

I was studying cinema at the Université Libre de Bruxelles (ULB) but even then my love for beer was greater than the love for cinema. Together with my friend and roommate Henry, we started brewing in the apartment where we lived in Rue de l'Ermitage in the municipality of Ixelles (hence the name of the brewery). François, who was studying in another faculty but who was in our group of friends, also brewed with us.

It was the now distant 2013 and at the brewery level again there was not much in Brussels except the Brasserie de la Senne and En Stomelings which were just beginning. There were no IPAs or new wave styles.

Step by step, we bought a 100-litre kit and started brewing in a cellar to develop more stable recipes. Our beer was already well regarded.

But we had other jobs. I moved to Canada for work, and there I discovered the amazing and rich Canadian beer scene, with so many brewpubs and beer bars. I found it extraordinary, better than the Belgian one.

When I returned to Brussels, I was full of ideas and enthusiasm, and I proposed to Henry and François that we start a professional project opening a craft brewery. It took us two years to launch the whole thing.

Between 2015 and 2016, we worked on the business plan. In 2016, we signed the contract for the building we are now in. However, there was a lot to fix and so we made an agreement with the Brasserie de Bastogne[7] to produce Lanterne, our first beer.

From 2017, we started brewing our beers here. Our philosophy is that we want to be 100% independent in terms of our production.

---

[7] Now Brasserie Minne.

***How did you choose this location? And why did you
choose to open a bar and beer shop?***

We wanted to find a place in Ixelles, a place to which we
are very attached to as we started brewing there. But it is a
very expensive municipality, there were no suitable
places, and the municipality did not help us.

When we found this place at the beginning, we weren't
very convinced as it is very big (and at the time we
weren't a big entity) and there was much to do to fix it.
But at the same time, it is not far from the centre, it is
close to the station (Gare du Midi) and to Brasserie
Cantillon. Therefore, it is in a strategic position.

The tap room in St. Gilles opened in 2019 and the Cave
de l'Ermitage (the beer shop) in 2021. Both projects are
part of our philosophy that aims to sell as much as
possible directly to our customers and to ensure that there
is as little distance as possible between producer and
consumer.

In addition, this tap room we are in is open only on
Fridays and Saturdays, it does not have a bar license
because it is a place of production. The function of the St.
Gilles bar is to have our beers available in a place very
close (less than two kilometres) to the production site. We
provide fresh beer to our tap room daily.

The goal behind the opening of the Cave de l'Ermitage
instead is to have a place to sell beers. People came here
but we didn't have the time and space to do it. In addition,
we needed space for the barrels, and we found it.

In addition to our beers at the Cave. We also sell beers of
breweries with which we make collaborations and natural
wines.

On which styles of beer do you focus on?

Our "core range" consists of four beers.

Our first beer was the Lantern, a very drinkable Pale Ale. La Soleil, a Wheat Ale Session with American hops. Belgians really love wheat beers, so we decided to revisit the style giving it some extra hops.

The Théorème de l'Empereur, a Pale Ale with Thè Jasmine, was initially not part of the range. There was a tea shop near where we started to brew, and we had a good relationship with the owners. We did a lot of experimentation. This went very well and was very much liked and so we decided to keep it in the core range.

The Noire du Midi, a porter, a style that we love very much and whose name is a tribute to the neighbourhood in which we brew.

We also produce several hoppy beers (IPA, Pale Ale), sour beers both with lactobacilli and with natural fermentation (Saison and Wild Beers). We also have several beers in barrels, so we need more and more space.

For a country of great beer tradition like Belgium is it possible to combine tradition with the innovations brought by craft breweries?

I find it a good thing that Belgium has a rich brewing tradition and many traditional styles. This allows people like us to experiment and work on the "new" styles.

Many breweries are characterised by the production of styles from other countries, such as the Brasserie de la Mule in Schaerbeek. The same thing happened in Canada and the United States. To be original, you need to be distinct.

As you are a few meters from a "giant" like Brasserie Cantillon, what is your relationship with them?

They are very kind and helpful to us. When we needed help, they always supported us. We collaborate with them when they organise the Quintessence hosting a "side event". Usually on Friday, they often come to have a beer here. They are nice, humble and kind people.

Do you think participating in a beer festival is an added value?

It depends. We don't go everywhere, we try to be selective. At festivals in Brussels, the goal is to bring new customers who can then come here to taste our beers. Abroad is different. We don't have enough volumes to export, so we participate to have fun, meet new people, have exchanges with other brewers and get known.

What about collaboration with other breweries?

Too often nowadays collaboration between breweries amounts to mere marketing operations without any real meaning. We collaborate only with people we know, and with whom there is a mutual appreciation of our work.

How do you think the Brussels beer scene will evolve in the coming years?

I believe that the number of breweries will continue to increase for a few years. It is a positive thing from one point of view. However, it is inevitable that sooner or later we will reach a level of saturation and then the real competition will begin.

Consumers are increasingly demanding. Breweries who produce quality products and have sufficient logistical capacity will survive. For the smaller ones, it won't be easy.

It's harder to sell today, harder than it was a few years ago. To succeed you have to build a reputation, to distinguish yourself.

You must remember that the number of microbreweries is growing but you that cannot encroach on the market share of large breweries. For example, in any bar with 8 tap system almost everywhere only one is dedicated to a small craft brewery. We all fight to be the one dedicated to the "small", while the other 7 remain the prerogative of the big industrial breweries. We have a lot of work to do to grow together.

What is your favourite beer from l'Ermitage?

It very difficult to answer, it depends on the season and the moment. Perhaps, the Lantern which is very drinkable and was the first we produced. But I really like mixed fermentation beers, saison and sours, the important thing is that they are low-grade.

What is your favourite beer from another Brussels brewery?

Taras Bulba of Brasserie de la Senne.

L'Annexe

Rue du Métal 19, 1060 St. Gilles

L'Annexe is a brewery\fermentery founded in 2017 in the municipality of St. Gilles by Grégoire Berthon and Max Lagrillière. The name "L'Annexe" comes from the building in which they make beer (L'Annexe of the Van der Kelen school).

It is one of the breweries of St. Gilles, located not far from the famous Parvis, and its vibrant beer scene.

When seen from the outside, the brewery looks like an old garage. It consists of two buildings; the first being the storage area and the tasting room. The second is the real brewery.

The reference style is the Saison but recently they started to produce non-alcoholic products such as very good lemonade.

They are open on Thursdays and Fridays from 5 pm to 8 pm.

Interview with Max Lagrillière

How and when did your adventure begin?

Gregoire and I are both from Brussels, and friends since childhood. We took separate professional paths. One evening, about ten years before we started with the brewery, we were drinking a beer and discussing how nice it would be to brew a beer ourselves. That same evening, we decided to sign up for the 20 km marathon of Brussels.

Since that day, we've been brewing beer regularly. We looked for a location in Brussels since we are both from here (I come from St. Gilles, Gregoire from Ixelles). Finding a place in St. Gilles was not easy, we searched in St. Gilles, Ixelles and Forest and finally we settled here.

You seem to have a particular preference for Saison's style, why?

We wanted to create a simple, not too bitter beer. We tried various yeasts and fell in love with Saison yeast.

We love the Saison, beers which are easy to drink but with so much character. We are very proud of our, Saison de Bruxelles, the first beer we produced, and which also won a gold medal at the Brussels Beer Challenge.

Are you planning to expand your range of beers?

We already have a range of six beers which is quite enough for our size. However, we produce temporary and seasonal beers and are working on alcohol free beer with the Janine brewery.

Does participation in a beer festival add value, in your opinion?

Recently, we were at Zythos Beer Festival. Participation in a beer festival first allows you to promote yourself. But it is hard to earn money in a beer festival. For a brewery of our size, it makes more sense to participate in a large festival than in a small or local one, in areas where our beers may not have yet arrived.

How did you deal with the pandemic?

Usually, in addition to the private sales we supply bars and restaurants with our organic beers and bio shops with our lemonades. Before the pandemic 65 % of our sales were of beers and 35 % of lemonade, now the reverse. The volume of beer sales has not decreased but the lemonade sales have increased. They are 100 % natural and fermented in the bottle, we are the only ones to do so.

How do you think the Brussels beer scene will evolve in the coming years?

The problem with Belgium is that there are so many good beers that people are not used to pay so much for a beer.

In Belgium, the margin for a bottle is lower than that of other countries. That is a great challenge for microbreweries. How can you sell a beer at a higher price than an Orval? It's only possible if you stay small and local.

Brussels is not London. There is no room for 30-40 breweries. Much will depend on the degree of ambition of the various breweries and the market share in Brussels they will tend to occupy. There is certainly no room for another Brasserie de la Senne or Brussels Beer Project. I think there is room for many brewpubs, there could be as many as 100.

What is your favourite beer from l'Annexe?

The Black Saison, it tastes like a Dry Stout. However, I drink more frequently the Saison de Bruxelles.

What is your favourite beer from another Brussels brewery?

I really like the Heavy Stout of No Science and the Brusseleir of Brasserie de la Senne.

Beerstorming[8]

Chau. d'Alsemberg 75, 1060 Saint-Gilles

Beerstorming is a very different project from the other Brussels breweries.

By booking and paying a fee, anyone can go there to create and produce their own beer. If the beer pleases a jury composed of experts and non-experts, the beer is produced on a large scale in a partner brewery (Brasserie Deseveaux, Brasserie Valduc or Brasserie Anders) and marketed on a large scale.

The production premises are quite small and are located in Chausse d'Alssemberg, in the heart of the municipality of St. Gilles and a few meters away from the Dynamo Bar.

Interview with Arthur Ries:

How and when did your adventure begin?

I studied international business but I have always had a passion for homebrewing. I founded Beerstorming with my father Olivier.

We wanted a brewery that was unique in its kind and that's why we decided to opt for a particular concept that would allow people to come and produce their own beer.

How did you choose this location?

---

[8] In May 2024, Beerstorming was put on sale.

We really like St. Gilles. It's a mix of different cultures, there are so many foreigners and many different cultures. Once upon a time, there were many breweries and we liked to bring one back. It is a beautiful area, not far from the centre, and improves day by day.

How does your project work?

This is a collaborative project. All our beers on the market have been processed, produced and selected by our audience.

Anyone can come to us to brew a beer; groups of friends, companies during team-building events or homebrewers. I, and the other brewers, guide them, explain the process and the potential of the different ingredients. Our brewing equipment allows you to make a brew of 75 litres at a time. Usually, we do two or three brews a week.

Every three months, the five beers that have been most appreciated during that period are submitted to a jury and the one that is judged the best is produced on large-scale by one of our partner breweries. They we launch it on the market.

How do you think the Brussels beer scene will evolve in the coming years?

I think there's still a lot of space. It is good that there is variety and innovation in this area.

Clearly, those who enter the market must offer something different in order to survive, they must have their own identity. In general, Belgium is a country that needs new models. It is a country that, from a beer point of view, is still too tied to its own traditions.

The same craft beer scene is still not sufficiently innovative. Today, the consumer is looking for something different. If we want to keep the name of "beer country" we have to change otherwise other countries will overtake us.

What's your favourite beer from Beerstorming?

Every time, I like to drink something different. At the moment, my favourite is the Peche-Moi Si Tu Peux, a very drinkable Berliner Weisse. Right now, I'm for sour beers.

What is your favourite beer from another Brussels brewery?

The Gueuze of Cantillon.

La Source

Rue Dieudonné Lefèvre 4, 1020 Brussels

La Source is a brewpub opened in October 2019 and located in the Laeken area in the BE-HERE complex, at the heart of the Beer Mile.

The BE-HERE is one of the most interesting places that has been developed in recent years in Brussels. It hosts productive activities related to eco-sustainable food, social and circular economy. On the beer side, beyond La Source, there is also Fermenthings.

Sitting in its beautiful terrace, you can drink with a view; kegs, tanks and barrels. It is a very nice place to relax and hang out.

They specialise in IPA, Sour&Wild, and barrel-aged beers. Beers are available directly on tap or on cans to take away, or drink on site. The owners are a couple; Mathieu Huygens and Nina Carleer.

The beer list is seasonal and constantly changing. There is a 20-tap system, 5 of which are installed directly on 600 litres tanks. They often organise concerts and food-beer matching events.

Mathieu welcomed me on a hot summer afternoon in his tap room. Together we talked about the La Source project and the future of beer in Brussels.

Interview with Mathieu Huygens

How and when did your adventure begin?

I am a graphic designer, like my wife Nina. I was tired of my work which I didn't consider to be creative enough. I learned how to make beer from the guys in the Brasserie de l'Ermitage. I started brewing beer at home once a week and I really enjoyed that. I saw it as very creative since I could play with tastes and aromas.

I continued like that for 4 or 5 years. Nina and I discussed how there were not yet any brewpubs in Brussels, and that it would be good if there were one where people could go and supply themselves directly "at the source". Hence the name of our Brewpub: "La Source" (in English "the source").

Our goal was to allow people drink as fresh a beer as possible; so, we decided to have a plant with 5 routes that could be supplied directly from our tanks.

A couple of years ago, Yannick of Fermenthings alerted us to this place at BE-HERE and proposed we open our brewpub here. We immediately liked the idea.

On which styles of beer do you focus on?

As homebrewer, I was very creative, and I am continuing with this approach. Here, we mainly produce sour beers and IPA. Last year, we produced more than 80 different beers, more than one per week. It is in our style to be creative and what characterises us is our recipes.

In the future we will also make Gruit, Imperial Stout and Lager.

Is there a particular brewery that inspired you?

I don't have a particular model. I like and respect many breweries. In Brussels, I respect the Brasserie de la Senne.

In general, I admire the American craft beer scene that combines research, quality and originality. From Other Half Brewing in New York, I tasted the best IPAs of my life.

`On a homebrewer evening, I tasted a sour gruit made by Tom of Antidoot that was phenomenal.

Do you have very nice labels, do you produce them?

My wife Nina, the co-founder of La Source. She takes care of the artistic side; I am the brewer and together we manage the administration.

She uses a lineography process. They are hand-printed and then finished on the PC. This is a long process.

In your opinion does participating in a beer festival add value?

This (2022) is the first year we regularly participated in beer festivals. We opened six months before the outbreak of the pandemic. This year we had the opportunity to attend the Firestone Beer Festival in Paso Roble, California, and then various beer festivals in Belgium. I'm not sure it's an added value but we enjoy it and have fun.

For a country of great beer tradition like Belgium, is it possible to combine tradition with the innovations brought by craft breweries?

That is what I am trying to do as a brewer. Having said that, Belgium, among the countries with a great brewery tradition, is the one that has moved more slowly towards new trends. If you look for Untapped, an app to rate beers, in countries such as France or Italy, you will immediately find the latest craft breweries. In Belgium you can still find Cantillon and Westvleteren.

I've been drinking beer since I was 12, I was drinking Chimay Blue at 16. I believe that we, Belgian brewers, have a great background to exploit having grown up drinking extraordinary products and non-industrial lagers.

At the same time, I believe that craft beers are sometimes too extreme and difficult to drink. The Belgian brewing tradition, made of easy-drinking beers, leads us brewers to produce quality, but easy to drink, beers. Among brewers, we often discuss the concept of "drinkability" and how to combine tradition and purity of flavours.

How do you think the Brussels beer scene will evolve in the coming years?

The current Brussels beer scene has many elements. There are breweries that focus on traditional styles, others which are more innovative. Right now, there are no more breweries focused on the same thing. The Brussels "beer public" is very open to novelties.

I think that there's plenty of room for brewpubs selling on site, as if they were a bar. I consider it more difficult to have other large breweries since the larger the brewery, the larger the volumes to be placed.

Having said that, the fact of producing "Belgian beers" in front of a certain section of the public helps, even if without the quality you do not go far.

We sell 30% of our products on site, and of the rest almost everything is sold in Brussels or elsewhere in Belgium. I think that for many breweries, foreign markets are an option.

In this area, in addition to La Source, there are En Stomelings, No Science and Brasserie de la Senne... do you think it can become a "Beer Mile" modelled on the London one?

I hope so, I would love it. Soon a road will open that connects this area directly to the Tour&Taxis area which will therefore facilitate the movement to and from the Brasserie de la Senne. For now, En Stomelings and No Science do not have real tap rooms. Brasserie de la Senne has limited hours. We have a good relationship with the other brewers in the area, and it would be nice that beer enthusiasts could move from one place to another.

What's your favourite beer from La Source?

I love Pigeon very much. It's a hoppy sour that characterises us. I can't say I invented the style, but we were the first to launch it and now I know with pleasure that many are trying to replicate it.

Pigeon is a fermented beer with yeast Kveik and Lactobacillus with Dry Hop by Sorachi Ale and Mosaic. It's an unusual beer that I'm very proud of.

The beer I drink the most is an IPA session, Carpe. IPA sessions are a style that I really like. For this beer is one of the most difficult to make, we have produced 11 different batches and I am not yet totally satisfied, I want it to be perfect.

La Jungle

Rue de la Petite Île 1A, 1070 Anderlecht

La Jungle is a microbrewery founded by a trio of friends (Felix, Martin and Christophe) and established within the socio-cultural project Studio Citygate in Anderlecht in the buildings of a former textile factory. It is a temporary arrangement that also includes a skate park, climbing installations, various craft workshops, and the Antidoote bar.

The location (temporary, in 2025 they will move while remaining in the territory of Brussels) is fascinating and certainly very alternative.

Their philosophy is to work to bring out the best potential of the ingredients they use (local cereals and European hops). The styles produced range from traditional Belgian ones such as Saison and Grisette to British styles (Porter, Golden Ale and Bitter) to spontaneous fermentations. Their flag beer is the Saison du Kanaal.

To understand more about it, I interviewed Christophe, one of the three founders.

Interview with Christophe Bravin:

Christophe, how and when did your adventure begin?

Together with Felix and Martin, we started brewing beer in November 2016. I remember we tried to make a winter beer in the style of Avec Les Bon Voeux of Brasserie Dupont.

Later we tried many different styles always using European hops. It was the time when IPAs and new wave beers in general were in vogue and we felt the need to produce traditional and easy-to-drink styles like the Saisons. In fact, it is the line that we still keep to in the brewery today.

In 2018, we decided to try to create a real brewery inspired by the magnificent brewpubs that we visited in Quebec and that are also in the USA. There was nothing like that in Brussels at the time.

We took our time, but things were moving slowly. So at the end of 2019 we decided to concentrate exclusively on this project.

We found a brewery in France selling its own equipment, which is what we are using now, and we found a space at the Hangar du Kanaal here in Anderlecht looking for projects like ours. It was a great solution because the rent was low and there was room for an outdoor bar for the summer.

Unfortunately, Covid came and slowed down the whole thing. We could only enter the brewery's premises one at a time and there was all the machinery to assemble. Everything was slow. Our goal was to produce a beer to serve during the summer in our bar space, but in those conditions, we would never have made it, and so we decided to produce it at En Stomelings brewery.

This is how our first beer, the Saison du Kanaal, was born. After the first brew at En Stomelings we started producing it in our brewery. Unfortunately, in December 2019, we were told that we had to move out. We needed funds to survive and so we went back to brew at En Stomelings.

In January 2021, we found our current location. Having arranged it, we started to brew. Finally, we had a place where we could concentrate 100 % of our production.

Unfortunately, it will not be our final location. The goal was to stay for at least two or three years, but it seems that in May 2023 this building will be demolished to make room for apartments.

We are looking for another location, in Brussels, in the municipalities of Forest or Anderlecht, to install our brewpub with a tap room and a depot for our barrels.

Which styles of beer do you focus on?

Our goal is to produce beers that are simple and drinkable. This is why we focus on styles such as Saison and Grisette, or on British styles such as bitter, porter and golden ale.

We aim to bring out all the potential of the ingredients we use, a bit like you do in Italian cuisine, in which each dish is made to highlight the characteristics of the different ingredients.

In particular, we work a lot on malts. We think that few breweries focus on the great potential of this fundamental ingredient. Generally, the focus is on hops or yeasts.

For example, with our bitter we tried to make cereals stand out a lot.

We also produce mixed fermentation beers with wild yeasts of mixed fruit stops and we are trying to make an oud bruin. We are inspired by De Ranke's productions. We're experimenting a lot.

Do you think participating in a beer festival is an added value?

It depends. There are two types of festivals: those "exhibitions" that look like fairs and those in which all breweries, large or small, are placed on the same level. In the latter, the brand counts less, and you meet many people, and you have the opportunity to promote your beers.

In any event, with beer festivals a brewery does not actually earn. Beer festivals serve as a promotion opportunity.

Among those in which we recently participated, I really enjoyed the BXL Beer Fest and the Wanderlust.

How do you think the Brussels beer scene will evolve in the coming years?

I think there is still room for growth. After all, as long as there are bars that serve exclusively Stella Artois, Maes or Jupiler, it means that there are still people to convince about the wealth of craft beers. One of our missions must be to try to "educate" the consumer.

Today, we have to act differently than 10 or 20 years ago. Before the aim of a brewery was to fit into the large-scale distribution. Now it's different and more complicated.

It's nice to find craft beers in a supermarket, but you cannot just survive like that. The Brewpub is a model that works, the important thing is to create your own personality.

What's your favourite beer from La Jungle?

The next one I have to brew. For the moment, I would say Mon Rêve, a "Wild" Grisette.

What is your favourite beer from another Brussels brewery?

The Gueuze of Cantillon and the Zinnebir of Brasserie de la Senne.

Brasserie de la Mule

Rue Rubens 95, 1030 Schaerbeek

The Brasserie de la Mule is one of the most interesting and particular additions to the Brussels beer scene. It is a brewery that produces almost exclusively German styles. It stands out in a country with a strong brewery tradition like Belgium.

Brasserie de la Mule opened in 2021, 60 years after Schaerbeek's last brewery (the Brasserie Roelants) had closed. It is located in a former tramway warehouse (Ecuries Van de Tram) a few steps from the Hotel de ville of Schaerbeek.

The tap room, the beating heart of the brewery, is open every day (except Tuesdays) from 16 to 23 (until midnight on the weekend).

I met Joel, founder and master brewer, to understand more about his project.

Interview with Joel Galy:

How and when did your adventure begin?

I started brewing at home with my mother when I was 14-15 years old. She's been doing it since the 1980s.

I worked in several bars and then started working at Brasserie de la Senne in 2014 for 6 years. Then for a few months in Cantillon, and finally in 2020 I opened my brewery.

How did you choose the name Brasserie de la Mule?

I choose it for several reasons. The mule is the symbol of the municipality of Schaerbeek.

In addition, the building in which we are located was a tramway warehouse, when the trams were towed by horses. The mule is the result of a donkey stallion mating with a female horse. Also, as you can see, I have a braid that looks like the tail of a mule.

How did you choose this location?

First of all, for the building. It has a beautiful terrace and is located in the centre of Schaerbeek. There were no breweries here for more than 60 years. Schaerbeek is like a small village where everyone more or less knows each other. I knew that such a project could work.

I also liked the idea of bringing a brewery back to this town after so many years. In the past there were many breweries.

More than a brewery, or brewpub, I like to call this place a neighbourhood bar. We often organise concerts twice a week. For me, beer is the means by which to create moments of conviviality. Here, you will not find flight with 5 cl tastings.

Have you chosen to focus mainly on German styles, for what reason?

I love German styles. It's a very wide beer scene with so many varieties ranging from Bock to Gose, from Lager to Alt. It's not just Pils.

In addition, no one makes German styles in Belgium anymore. In the 1960s, many lagers were produced in

Brussels, but they slowly disappeared, supplanted by Belgian or English styles.

I think, I'm the only one in Belgium to focus on German styles.

When you start a business, you must try to offer something different to differentiate yourself in the market. Many of my colleagues do dozens of IPAs or Imperial Stouts, I was not interested in competing on these styles.

In addition, I really like the way Germans drink beers. When you enter a bar or a place you immediately get a good beer, easy to drink, and that allows you to focus on the moment and the people you are with. They are "social" beers, they help to socialise. There are 9-degree beers made with 10 different hops that are complicated just to think about.

Do you have other German styles in your pipeline?

I'll brew an Alt and then a Bock soon. Then there are so many to do; Double Bock, Rauch...

In my range, I also have non-German styles like Saison or Tropical Lager.

Four new fermenters have just arrived. I used to produce 1000 hectolitres a year and I had no room to produce anything else. In addition, I didn't want to be one of those breweries that produces a new beer every week. I want to offer my customers a stable range of beers.

Do you think participating in a beer festival is an added value?

I take part in many beer festivals, maybe too many. Both in Belgium and abroad. I just got back from the Beer

Village. It was great. I'll also organise an Oktoberfest here at the brewery. Beer festivals do not allow you to make money, they are useful to make contact with customers, retailers and to get to know other brewers.

My ideal beer festival, however, is not the one where you drink a 12 cl beer and then switch to another stand. I like much more models like the Beer Village in Italy where in addition to beers there is good music and good food.

This allows you to approach a wider audience than the usual one of beer enthusiasts.

How do you think the Brussels beer scene will evolve in the coming years?

When I started working at Brasserie de la Senne, there were only two breweries in town. And for many years before, there was only one. We're still at the beginning. Now there are eighteen breweries in Brussels plus many beer firms.

There's still a lot of room. Not for large breweries like Brasserie de la Senne or the Brussels Beer Project, but for brewpubs like mine, La Source, or L'Ermitage.

Brewpub is a winning model in the world, not just here. I think it's the only option to survive if it opens up at this historical moment. The heart of the brewery is the bar.

In your book, there is also a beer tour for each neighbourhood. Each neighbourhood has its own history and peculiarity. People from St. Gilles seldom move to Schaerbeek to go for a drink but circulate in St. Gilles. And it is so too the for the beer drinkers of Schaerbeek.

That's why the local dimension matters a lot, that's what people want now. Four years ago, the people who lived in Laeken, Forest and Schaerbeek went downtown to Brussels for a drink. Now there are many "local" places.

And then look at what happened in London or Paris. In Paris during the last three years the beer scene literally exploded. There was nothing before.

What's your favourite beer from Brasserie de la Mule?

It depends on the time of year and also the time of day. I really like Helles. But I only make beers that I like to drink. Generally speaking, I love Schneider Weisse.

What is your favourite beer from another Brussels brewery?

Taras Bulba of Brasserie de la Senne. But there are so many good beers. It depends about the moment.

DrinkDrink!

Rue Paepsem 123, 1070 Anderlecht

Drink-Drink! is a project of three friends from Brussels: Pierrick Couvreur, Frédéric Lefebvre and Jean Van den Broeck. They have in common two passions: beer and bicycles.

They began, like many, to brew in a cellar (Jean's), and produced their first beer at the Saint-Lazare brewery, then opening in their own site in the municipality of Anderlecht, in an industrial area.

They often organise concerts on site. For the moment, the brewery does not have real opening hours.

They focus on producing low-grade organic beers, ideal for cyclists. To understand more, I went to their brewery/tap room to interview the brewer, Jean.

Interview with Jean Van den Broeck:

How and when did your adventure begin?

I've been brewing at home since my university years. I got a Master's degree in Science and I have some knowledge of chemistry. For years, I worked in a different field than beer.

Five years ago, Pierrick, one of my associates, who owned two organic grocery stores, told me that in Belgium there were only "classical" styles for organic beers and IPAs and low fermentation beers were missing. So, we decided to try. At first it was a leisure project, now all three of us are full time.

Why did you choose the name Drinkdrink! ?

We are three cyclists, great fans of "two wheels". The name recalls the sound of the bicycle bell and adapts well to a beer.

What types of beer do you produce?

Our three basic beers are Biciclette, Pale Ale, Tandem, White IPA and BMX, an IPA. We produce them at Anders brewery. Here on site, we produce more beers in lower volumes; the Folding, an IPA Session, Cuistax, a Hoppy White Lager, Gravel, a NEIPA, and Cargo, a stout we do in collaboration with the torrefaction activity we have here in front. The goal is to have all the production here on site within 5 years.

Do you think participating in a beer festival is an added value?

I believe that participating in a beer festival offers different opportunities such as meeting people, especially other brewers, and promoting the brand. I enjoy discussions with the fans of my beers. We've been to Zithos recently.

How do you think the Brussels beer scene will evolve in the coming years?

I'm pretty optimistic. I have the impression that my competitors are not the other Brussels breweries but the giants such as AB Inbev, Heineken... the big industrial groups in general. In Belgium, the market share occupied by craft beers is lower than in other European countries and much lower than that of the USA. There is so much work to do in this respect.

In addition, the mind-set of customers is changing and there are many bars that no longer want to have only industrial beers.

What's your favourite beer from DrinkDrink?

The biciclette. It is an "every day" beer, hopped, but not too much and very refreshing.

What is your favourite beer from another Brussels brewery?

The Taupe of La Source.

Brasserie Surréaliste

Pl. du Nouveau Marché aux Grains 22-23,
1000 Brussels

One of the most interesting novelties in the city centre, in the vibrant district of Dansaert, is undoubtedly the Brasserie Surrealiste.

The Grison brothers, Edward (the brewer) and Charles (the creative one), opened this new brewpub in April 2022 in an iconic 1932 Art Deco building that was formerly a banana warehouse. Aesthetically it is a unique brewery with a real surrealist style. The tap room is elegant and spacious while the production site is located in the basement.

Currently, it opens from Thursday to Saturday from 6 p.m. to 2 a.m. On site, you can buy their beers, it is one of the different Brussels breweries that has opted to make them only in cans.

Brasserie Surrealiste specialises in IPA and sours beers.

I interviewed the two brothers to discuss their impressive project.

Interview with Charles and Edward Grison:

Charles and Edward Yorick, how and when did your adventure begin?

Edward: I started as a homebrewer in 2015, I loved the classic Belgian styles but wanted to experiment with new styles. I travelled a lot in the USA and Canada, where I was in excellent breweries which inspired me.

Charles: I don't make beer, I drink it. In the team, I deal with marketing and communication. We worked on the project to open a brewpub for 5 years.

We wanted a location that was special, which in addition to brewing beer would allow us to cook, play music and organise parties. The research lasted about a year and a half.

Why did you choose to call it "Brasserie Surrealiste"?

Charles: The term "Surrealists" is deeply linked to Brussels and Belgium, a country of great surrealist artists. I personally love art and especially surrealist artists.

Besides making beer, we wanted to create a place with references to surrealist art. I always had the idea of a place that would attract not just beer lovers. In Belgium, although there are excellent beers, there are no iconic places to drink them, there are no places with references to art.

What types of beer do you produce?

Edward: For the moment we focus on hoppy beers and classic sour beers. I like to play with hops, experiment and feel the difference. I want to explore the world of wild sours soon. But we are a brewpub, and we need a wide range. That's why I also produced other styles like Stouts or Lagers.

For a country of great beer tradition like Belgium is it possible to combine tradition with the innovations brought by craft breweries?

Edward: For us, small breweries, it is impossible to compete with traditional Belgian beers. The Belgian market is full of excellent and yet inexpensive beers. There are also generational differences, for example, our parents love traditional Belgian beers.

We turn to a different market segment, that of traditional beer enthusiasts. People who want to try different styles from the classic Blonde or Triple and who are willing to spend more on it. We also operate in Brussels, which is a different market in comparison with the rest of Belgium.

Do you think participating in a beer festival is an added value?

Edward: I believe that beer festivals are an opportunity to make us known and reach different customers. Obviously, it depends on the particular beer festival. Some are also an opportunity to meet and exchange ideas with other brewers, to establish future collaboration. It is one of our aims in the coming months.

How do you think the Brussels beer scene will evolve in the coming years?

Charles: There is always room for those who produce good quality beers. The market in Brussels is wide and there are so many people interested in craft beers and willing to pay more for them than maybe a classic Belgian beer. The determining factor is and will be the quality that beer enthusiasts know how to recognise.

What is your favourite beer from Brasserie Surrealiste?

Charles: Blackcurrant and Raspberries Sour Ale. Unfortunately, it's finished, if not, I'd let you taste it.

Edward: I love that question. At the moment, the Dream in Mosaic, a single hop IPA with mosaic hops. But if you ask me the same question in a month, I will probably have changed my mind. In general, I love pale ale.

What is your favourite beer from another Brussels brewery?

Charles: I love the complexity of Cantillon's Gueuze and 3 Fonteinen. In addition, for those like us living in Brussels, they are easy to find and relatively cheap.

Edward: There are a lot of them. I'd say the Fou Fone by Cantillon.

Mazette

Pl. du Jeu de Balle 50, 1000 Brussels

Mazette is a brewpub located in the famous Place du Jeu de Balle, in the old building "Skieven Architek". It a cooperative brewpub that combines the production of beer with that of other non-alcoholic products, bread and dishes with seasonal products. The focus is on around sustainability and they strictly use only Belgian products.

Currently, the cooperative has more than 700 members divided into four categories. The first category is "Les Marolliens", the inhabitants of the neighbourhood. The second "Les Zwanzeurs" are the customers of the brasserie. Then there are the "Architeck" who are the partner associations and finally the "Frucheleers" who are the workers of the cooperative.

Decisions are taken at a general meeting in which each member has a vote, without distinction of category.

The beers they produce are consumed only on site, as they are not bottled. The only beer constantly available is the Suur de Bruxelles, a sour beer made with natural yeast (Surette). The others are variable. On tap there are also beers from other Brussels breweries, ciders (selected by Cidroteque Joranin Schaerbeek) and other non-alcoholic products produced on site (Kombucha, lemonade and cold tea).

Once you enter, you immediately notice the brewing equipment and the kitchen (with a wood burning oven). At the back, there is a nice terrace.

Mazette is one of the latest arrivals on the Brussels beer scene having opened in March 2022. At the moment, they are open in the evening during the week and from 10 am until evening during the weekend. In the future, they plan to open for lunch.

To understand more about the project, I interviewed Mazette's brewer (and baker), Yorick.

Interview with Yorick Coomans:

How and when did your adventure begin?

I started about 15 years ago, I wasn't at the age to drink beer yet. I was quite fascinated by the brewing process and I started producing it thanks to, and with, my mother. One day, she gave me a kit and asked me to make a beer for her. In fact, I learned by myself.

Subsequently, I studied bioengineering at the university and this gave me the opportunity to have a scientific understanding about the production processes for food and drink.

After my studies, I worked in the food industry in a dairy farm for a couple of years. I then moved to Brussels. Originally, I lived about thirty kilometres from the city in Wallonia. In Brussels, I started brewing at the Beerstorming brewery. I produced small volumes (80 litres) but more than the 20 litres I had been used to with the kit.

Later, I worked in a bakery to learn how to make bread. I have always been passionate about the process of food transformation, from solid to liquid, or from liquid to solid as with cheese.

Then I went abroad. I travelled a lot by bike with my girlfriend. We were in many farms where I saw with my own eyes the food "at the source", I saw how it is produced, the processes and sacrifices that are made.

After my return to Brussels, and with some guys I knew from before the trip (the other founding partners Pierre, France and Boris), we decided to start working on the project of a cooperative Brewpub. We had long thought about what to do and especially how to do it.

We gave ourselves three guidelines; produce on-site products for sale on site only, develop a type of premises that respond to the needs of post-pandemic market, and involve our suppliers and customers in the project. This is how the decision arose to create a cooperative in which we cooperate in establishing working conditions and in which suppliers of our products and the people of the neighbourhood participate in the decisions.

We decided to call ourselves "Mazette" which in French is an expression that denotes something surprising. It is also the name of a small bird, the little seagull, to which we dedicated the logo.

How did you choose this location?

We considered different options. Marolles is a place we all love. It is the beating heart of Brussels, a multicultural symbol. It is the emblem of this city with many economic, social and cultural differences. One of our goals is to bring all these people from different backgrounds to our brewpub.

What types of beer do you produce?

Our flag beer is the Suur de Bruxelles, the only beer we always have on tap and that will always be available.

It's a sour beer, I like to call it a "terroir" beer because it is made with local ingredients. Barley and malt come from the region of Liège, the hops from the region of Namur. Both are produced by cooperatives that promote regenerative agriculture. We also use bread yeast.

The use of completely natural ingredients, produced without excessive exploitation of the soil, is the characteristic that distinguishes each of our products.

As for the other beers, we like to brew both classic styles and "new" styles. At the moment, we have 4 tanks, but the goal is to reach 10. Every time a tank is empty, we fill it with a different beer.

Do you think participating in a beer festival is an added value?

We have a very innovative model for Brussels as we produce and sell entirely on site. For our model therefore the answer is no. I do not rule out that in the future we might participate in some local festivals in Brussels. For now, we just wish to achieve some stability.

How do you think the Brussels beer scene will evolve in the coming years?

It depends on which model a brewery chooses to adopt. There is room for craft beers in Brussels, and there is room to change people's mentality about it.

First of all, we need to change the consumption pattern. Today, 70 % of the market in Belgium is dominated by three large companies.

Clearly in Brussels there is no room to have ten breweries like Brasserie de la Senne or the Brussels Beer Project, they are too big to replicate.

Then there is the environmental dimension. Does it make sense to have large producers who have to export?

I think there's plenty of room for small-volume microbreweries and brewpubs. I believe in the brewpub model. I believe that 50% of bars in Brussels theoretically could produce their own beer, even in very small volumes. It would be great if the Brussels of the past could return. And with lower transport costs, lower environmental impact, you could bypass marketing and reduce energy consumption. We would have a more sober development model. I think brewpub is the model of the future for Brussels, the beer capital.

We work with this objective; bring people closer to this model, bring customers close to the producer by letting them understand how to brew beer. Industries have created a wrong image of this world.

What is your favourite beer from Mazette?

Without doubt, the Suur de Brussels. A beer is not only drunk for how it is made, but also for what it represents. All my passion is in this beer.

What is your favourite beer from another Brussels brewery?

I love Cantillon's beers. I like their approach, although they are famous all over the world, they are still a family brewery. They are simple people who like to talk to their customers, describe their beers and explain their philosophy. I would say Rosé de Gambrinus.

Brasserie iLLegaal

Rue Bollinckx 300, 1190 Forest

Brasserie iLLegal is one of the most curious and alternative locations of the city brewery scene. It is to be found at the border between the Region of Brussels and the Flemish Brabant, in the municipality of Forest

Getting there is not easy without a car. You need to take bus number 73 from Gare du Midi. In the surroundings there are also the Brasserie Drogenbos (a very interesting entity not included in this book for purely geographical reasons) and the brewery Lambiek Fabriek (one of the most interesting producers of Lambic-Gueuze among those that emerged recently).

It is one of many beer firms that have become independent in recent years. The building is very nice and spacious, and often hosts concerts from the underground and alternative music scene.

Here beer is a tool to support cultural projects, on site or in other places in the city.

I went there for a chat with their brewer, Emile.

Interview with Emile Piret:

How and when did your adventure begin?

I'm quite new to the craft beer world. Until three and a half years ago, I was a drinker of Stella Artois and had never tried a Gueuze.

When I finished university, I couldn't find a job and so I started working in a bar. That brought me closer to this world. I started to become curious about the beers I served and I began to inform myself about everything behind it... from the ingredients to the background of the various producers, as well as of course tasting them.

I also started brewing at home, along with my father, who already had it as a hobby. We were brewing abbey beers, with a quite high alcohol level.

This new passion has changed my life. I decided to take a professional course on how to make beer at the EFP/SFPME here in Brussels.

Later, I worked at En Stomelings and Brasserie de la Mule.

Beer is the emblem of being Belgian, it is part of our "terroir", it is our pride, our tradition, our history.

Brewing is a craft profession but at the same time creative and intellectual. Previously, I did not know to choose a beer. Brewing beer touches all three aspects. I especially love this aspect of my work.

Tell me more about iLLegal project.

I'm new to the team. The project began in 2016 when Axel, along with other guys including Thomas and Joe, created an ASBL. They started brewing beer to sell it to their friends. They used their proceeds to invest in and support cultural projects. They made beer at the Belgo Sapiens brewery in the Walloon Brabant and at the Jandrain-Jandrenouille brewery.

Beer has always been a means to support cultural projects.

The created their recipes and they also had a mini brewplant with which they experimented.

This location is quite recent, we have been here for a year. There was almost nothing here. Most of the machines arrived in January 2022. They assembled everything on their own. I've been here since March 2022. They needed a professional brewer. We met on a bowling field and they asked me to work with them. I'm the only one who deals with the beer side. The rest of Illegal's team is focused on cultural projects.

Illegal rather than being a brewery is a cultural association, beer is not the end but a means to support cultural projects and bring people together.

You have a very big location, what kind of activities do you organise?

Indeed, we have a lot of space. From April 2022, we started hosting concerts, theatre performances and organising music festivals.

We host many local music groups, especially from the alternative music scene. The program will become more and more intense.

We are trying to figure out what are the best times for our audience. We are rather far from the city, which is an advantage because we can organise parties that last until late, but at the same time it is not easy to reach us.

What kind of beers do you produce?

I'm also trying to determine what our audience likes. We have two small fermenters that allow me to experiment.

Right now, we produce the three "historic" beers from the Illegal range, which I have adapted a bit.: Sociaal, a hoppy lager, Illegal, a golden IPA, and the Khop Killer, a NEIPA.

Our beers are all in cans and the labels are designed by local artists.

I really love barrel aged and I own an orchard near Namur, so I do not rule out that in the future we may produce other styles.

Do you think participating in a beer festival is an added value?

Honestly, I'm not a big fan of beer festivals. Of course, I like to meet other brewers and taste new beers. For the moment, participation in beer festivals is not the priority of the Illegal team.

If one day we do participate in a festival, it will be at a "popular" festival.

This does not mean that we do not like to meet other breweries. Last year, we invited other breweries for a bowling tournament, it was a very interesting and fun day.

How do you think the Brussels beer scene will evolve in the coming years?

I think there's still room for other projects, but it all depends on how everyone decides to structure their business. At this precise moment, having the opportunity to serve and sell beer on site is crucial. The model for the next few years is the Brewpub. Right now, I see little space for breweries trying to emulate the Brasserie de la

Senne, or En Stomelings; while I see space for models such as the Brasserie de la Mule.

What is your favourite beer from iLLegal?

A beer that you can't taste here. An IPA that we have brewed for Recyclart, a cultural project in Molenbeek. I only used European hops (Mistral and Hallertau) and it is sold only by them.

Among those that we have here, Sociaal. I love the Pils and I want to try to make it more and more better.

What is your favourite beer from another Brussels brewery?

Brussels Calling by Brasserie de la Senne.

Co-Hop — Brussels Cooperative Brewpub

Chau. de Wavre 950, 1040 Etterbeek

Co-Hop is one of the most recent projects on the Brussels beer scene.

It impressed me a lot for two essential reasons. The first is that it is the city's first cooperative brewery. The second is the fact that it brought together four breweries created by boys, and girls, united by the desire to revolutionise the world of beer while knowing, and respecting, the traditions.

It is located in Etterbeek, in the historic site of the Arsenal, between offices, residential buildings and not far from VUB University.

The project was born from the iniative of Thomas (Brasserie Witloof) who involved Rémi and Adrien (DrinkThatBeer, now coordinator of Co-Hop's bar and manager respectively), Morane (Janine) and Gilles (1B2T).

It is an innovative, supportive and eco-responsible model. The brewery is equipped with a heat recovery system, solar panels and in the future it will be equipped with a system to recover the Co2 produced during fermentation.

Each brewery produces and takes care of its range using three fermenters (out of 15). The remaining three are used to produce Co-Hop branded beers or to allow other brewers, without breweries, to brew their own beers.

All the beers produced on site are on can, the Co-Hop branded beers are classic styles and with a neutral label, to differentiate themselves from the products of the founding breweries.

There is also a tap room (opened in September 2022 and open from Tuesday to Saturday) with a 24-tap system: 5 each for the 4 breweries, 3 for Co-Hop beers and one for a guest brewery.

Each brewery member of the project has shared its knowledge and talents with the others. Visiting Co-Hop you can breathe a positive air of cooperation, complicity and desire to emerge in the fantastic world of Brussel beer scene.

Brasserie Witloof

Thomas is the founder of the Co-Hop, as well as the first stakeholder of the project that I interviewed. Together, we discussed this innovative project and much more.

Interview with Thomas Detorube:

How and when did your adventure begin?

I'm a professional cameraman. I have many friends who work in different bars that, over the years, have allowed me to taste several very good beers. I'm a guy who likes to do things by myself and so I've started brewing beers in my Evere kitchen in October 2015.

One day a friend who owns an art gallery in central Brussels, Calaveras, and who lived in Mexico for two years asked me to create a chilli beer to serve during a vernissage in his gallery. So this is how the Santa Calaveras Chiplotes-les came into being and its remarkable success made me think of the idea of marketing it. I started to brew 200 litres at the Brasserie Valduc where I stayed for three years.

From 2020, the idea of launching a cooperative came to my mind. In 2016, I tried to launch another project, Brasserette. It was a project that would give amateur brewers the opportunity to come to us to make their own beer and meet other brewers. Unfortunately, due to lack of experience, we have not been able to achieve that.

But the idea stayed in my mind. I always wanted to create a brewery but I didn't feel able to do it myself. That's why

I decided to launch this cooperative model, which strengthens you and helps to share risks. In January 2020, I launched the idea of the project on several Facebook groups of amateur brewers. Having received several positive responses, I organised the first meeting where a dozen people participated.

The guys from DrinkThatBeer were the most motivated and we decided to start together. They also involved Janine into the project. Later, 1Bière2Tartines joined. I know Gilles a long time and he was also involved with the Brasserette project.

Then Covid came and slowed down the project. We visited and evaluated several facilities in Uccle and in the city centre. Finally, we opted for this location. It's a former chocolate factory. We believe in the potential of the area. There are no major bars, we are close to the university and many offices.

We bought the brewing equipment in China. The price included consultation input from the company's engineers for the assembly. Unfortunately, as their COVID vaccines were not recognised by Europe, they could not come. So, we put it all together by ourselves.

We had our first brew in April 2022. Everyone has their own beers that they produce in their own fermenters. We have fifteen tanks and each brewery has a 20-litre fermenter and two 10 litres. The other three are dedicated to the beers we produce as a Co-Hop brand and to beer firms. We have all been beer firms or gipsybrewers and so we wanted to offer others this possibility.

We have also decided that the four of us will remain as the only brewery members of the cooperative because if the numbers increase then it is going to be difficult to make decisions. However, we have opened up to capital to other co-operators who can come to follow a brewing course. We organise courses in English and French.

Why did you choose the name Witloof?

I lived in Evere, I was looking for a name with a Brussels identity. At first, since I was brewing in another brewery outside Brussels, I didn't want to call it by a name that would recall a commune or a neighbourhood of Brussels. It would have been like lying to my clients. Evere housed a market where the chicory witloof (or Belgian endive) was sold. The witloof chicory is also bitter and recalls the bitterness of beer.

What kind of beers do you produce?

As with Witloof, I want to do something different, not traditional styles. I've always loved classic styles like Triple but now I want something different. From the beginning, I was inspired by products from breweries such as De Ranke and Brasserie de la Senne that make excellent beers. I want beers that are interesting for the palate; modern beers.

I currently have four beers in my range: Boentje, Rye Pale Ale, Chipote-LesSaison, No Pal, IPA Session and Saison Sichuan, Dark Saison with Sichuan pepper and Coyote, a juicy IPA. I like to use unconventional spices.

As Co-Hop, we have chosen to make sober labels and styles that do not follow those produced by those breweries who are part of the cooperative.

Do you think participating in a beer festival is an added value?

It's a way to make yourself known. For now as Witloof and also as Co-Hop we have participated in local festivals. In the future, maybe we will also organise a festival.

How do you think the Brussels beer scene will evolve in the coming years?

I hope there will be room for everyone. Many of us dream of succeeding in this world, but clearly it is complicated. We live in a difficult period, first the COVID pandemic, then the increase of the prices raw materials and energy. But this is the case for everyone, we are all in the same boat.

I think it's better for everyone to have a wider choice. For this, we must all thank the Brasserie de la Senne, who has paved the way for all of us, in Brussels and in Belgium.

Covid has changed the strategies of many breweries. First, we tried to "colonise" the bars, then the bars closed and many didn't know where to sell anymore, many of those who said "never my beers in a supermarket" had to re-think that approach.

Personally, I believe that finding craft beers in a supermarket is a good thing. Other countries are ahead on this issue, in Belgium we are behind.

What is your favourite beer from Witloof?

It depends on the moment. Now I would say Boentje, I drink it very easily.

What is your favourite beer from another Brussels brewery?

I love the products of La Source.

1 Biére 2 Tartines (1B2T)

Gilles has travelled and lived abroad a lot. He translated his passion into his beers and has given them exotic names and ingredients. Here's, my interesting chat with the founder of 1B2T.

Interview with Gilles Bastin:

How and when did your adventure begin?

I am a bio-engineer and have always been passionate about craft beer. In Louvain-la-Neuve, I always participated in the Quinzaine de la Bière, a fantastic event- but very focused on the classic Belgian beers. At the time, I together with friends of the same mind I wished to try new styles of beer.

I lived and worked in the Democratic Republic of Congo in Lubumbaschi for two years. There, I started brewing many recipes. There was a proposal for me to create a brewery on site, but at the time I did not have the necessary experience.

I loved my work in Africa. It allowed me to travel all over the Black Continent and I also learned new methods of brewing. I returned to Belgium in 2016 and I worked for two and a half years for AB-Inbev as Chef Line Manager following the production process step by step. After that, I worked for another Belgian company dealing with cleaning products for the agri-food industries.

While working for AB-Inbev I created 1B2T in 2018. I wanted to produce the recipes I had created in Africa and see if the people would appreciate them.

I started brewing at the Jandrain-Jandrenouille brewery. The first beer I made was Mermaide, a White IPA, which was quite successful. The intent was to open a brewery by myself within two years, but Covid complicated everything.

Thomas of Witloof proposed the Co-Hop project to me. We had already tried together to launch the Brasserette project in 2016, that unfortunately that did not work.

What does the expression "1 bière, c'est 2 tartines...!" mean?

It is a classic Belgian expression widely used in our grandparent's time. It is linked to the saying "where the brewer goes, the baker doesn't go". It means that when you drink a beer, your stomach is full. Remember that, at the time beers were always very strong in alcohol.

I chose this expression because I like it a lot and everyone in Belgium knows it.

What kind of beers do you produce?

I have a clear line; each of my beers is dedicated to a different region of the world. I have travelled a lot and have relatives who live around the world, I know many different cultures. I want people to travel through my beers, savouring different tastes.

The first is Mermaid, a white IPA. The name is a tribute to a Flemish legend that tells of the sailors of the Scandinavian ships, who in order to reach the Bay of Biscay had to pass by the North Sea, and were seduced by the song of the sirens. There is a statue in Ostend dedicated to a mermaid.

The second is the Mwana Abyssa, an African hoppy ale made with hibiscus and inspired by Bissap, a West African beverage based on hibiscus. Then there is the Guru, a "Spiritual" spiced ale, with coriander and cardamom. It is dedicated to India.

The newest are Saison&Seizonen, a Belgian farmhouse ale, inspired by the Saisons of Wallonia, and the lesser-known ones of the Flanders. It is a tribute to Belgium and its regions.

Then the Nightrider, a West Coast IPA with American hops, and TechnoKviking, an IPA with Kveik yeast inspired by a famous Youtube video in which a boy dressed as a Viking dances techno music.

The last one is the ak Khunn -Milkshake Asian Sour.

In the coming months, I will produce a Berliner Weisse and an Imperial Stout.

Do you think participating in a beer festival is an added value?

It's a way to make yourself known. In the future we will participate as Co-Hop at festivals. You don't make money, but you make a lot of contacts. It is also a way to spread craft beers. I have noticed, at several festivals that I have attended, that there are so many people interested in new styles, not just young people or beer geeks.

How do you think the Brussels beer scene will evolve in the coming years?

I think there's still room for other projects. In Etterbeek, for example, we are the only one.

Brussels is a city in turmoil, there is also a sort of "Route des Brasseurs" (Belgian Beer Mile) in the Tour&Taxis area.

Having a brewpub or a brewery equipped with a tap room is crucial. In 2022, without a tap room it would be difficult to survive. Everybody is doing it. A brewery without a taproom might have many challenges in the future. It is also essential to have a clear project with a proper identity.

What is your favourite beer from 1B2T?

At the moment, the Mermaid. However, I like a lot also the TechnoKviking.

What is your favourite beer from another Brussels brewery?

The Berliner Weisse by Brasserie de la Mule.

DrinkThatBeer

DrinkThatBeer[9] was born from the idea and the passion for beer of three friends Matthieu, Adrien and Remy. It all started from a discussion at Place Flagey in September 2017 that led to the three deciding to make beer. They started at home, then at Jandrain-Jandrenouille and finally they joined as founders the Co-Hop project.

To discover more about them, I met with Matthieu, another real globetrotter who, from Singapore to Etterbeek, passing through France, who showed me this great project.

Interview Mathieu Alan:

How and when did your adventure begin?

I have a master's degree in mechanics, I am an engineer. I worked for big car manufacturers for about ten years traveling between France, Belgium and Germany.

Then I met my girlfriend and decided to go live in Singapore. In the meantime, the adventure of DrinkThatBeer began.

I had a year and a half sabbatical in Singapore where I dedicated my body and soul to brewing beer. In Singapore, there is quite a special atmosphere for brewing, since there it is almost always 30 degrees.

Ingredients such as yeasts, hops and malt are very expensive to obtain. I read many books about beer. I

---

[9] In 2024, they opened a tap room in St.Gilles.

watched many videos. I also joined a group of local home brewers together with whom we purchased yeasts to share the cost.

Then, Covid came. There was a brutal lockdown in Singapore. In the meantime, I was looking for work in several breweries; first in Singapore, where it was very difficult to get a work visa, and then in Hong Kong and Australia.

We enjoyed our life in Singapore, and we wanted to stay. Nevertheless we also wanted to continue travelling.

Unfortunately, I didn't find a job and so we returned to Europe. I found a job as a brewer at a brewery in Marcoussy, in the south of the Paris region. I worked there for a year; a very formative experience. It was a family brewery, I learned different approaches than those I was used to. It was also a quite successful brewery and I witnessed its growth.

But the Co-Hop project was waiting for me. From Singapore, I hadn't followed it much, my partners Remy and Adrian, took care of it. When I returned to Brussels, while helping to develop the project, I worked as a brewer for a year at the Belgoo brewery. I left my job there at the end of the summer to devote myself completely to Co-Hop. I have so many ideas which I can't wait to implement.

Where does the name "DrinkThatBeer" come from?

With Remy and Adrian, the other two members of DrinkThatBeer, we often argue and yell at each other. It sounds like "Shut up, sit down, and drink your beer". In fact, it is simply "Drink that fucking beer" but please do not write it!

What kind of beers do you produce?

Before we started brewing here in Co-Hop, we were gypsy brewers and we brewed our beers at the Jandrain-Jandrenouille brewery.

Our range includes the Barbe Rousse, a Belgian IPA, the Grand-Mere, a wheat beer, the Mitch, an Indian pale lager made using as a model the California Common Beer, and Framboo, a sour, the only sour beer from Co-Hop.

The next one will be a NEIPA, the Naya.

Do you think participating in a beer festival is an added value?

For us, it is a way to promote and promote Co-Hop. We have participated in several festivals in Wallonia, and in some small festivals in Brussels.

How do you think the Brussels beer scene will evolve in the coming years?

Brussels and Belgium are multicultural places where so many traditions meet and mix. I really value Belgium's beer tradition. But I think there is room for novelties, because there are so many new people who have lived in so many places and who want to try different things. Beer is creativity, the new generation wants novelties and surprises. Of course, tradition must be protected because it is history, experience, work. Then everything is a cycle and sooner or later the tastes change.

I think that right now the model to focus on is the Brewpub. Not having a brewpub means having to produce a lot and sell as much to make a profit. Nowadays, if you sell only to bars, the margins have been reduced a lot.

Someone has done it in the past in Brussels. The Brussels Beer Project did so, and now they have opened a tap room in Anderlecht.

Producing in Brussels is rather expensive, it helps greatly to have the opportunity to sell directly on site. Having a tap room allows the brewer to have direct contact with the customer, to be able to present the product, explain it to him... the task of a brewer is not only to make beer but also to explain to people why and how to make a beer. Education is important. Because beer is a product with a process and a story behind it.

What is your favourite beer from DrinkThatBeer?

The Framboo. It's very balanced, I would dare to define it as "gourmet".

What is your favourite beer from another Brussels brewery?

Orange Gruit by La Source. I really like the products of this brewery and I very much with their philosophy.

Janine

Janine is a brewery\bakery. The project was born from the idea of Bertrand, Morane and Maxine. Their main goal is to fight against food waste. Unsold bread, grains and excess yeast are used to produce beers. The project won the Greenlab Incubator Audience award in 2020.

Morane is also one of the few women working as a brewer in a Brussels brewery. To learn more about their interesting project, I interviewed her.

Interview with Morane Le Hiress:

How and when did your adventure begin?

I started brewing at home in 2017. I used to be a researcher in biology. When my contract expired, I decided to change my life. I took a course to become a brewer in Nancy and then I did internships in several breweries.

I arrived in Brussels in 2020 with my partner, I had previously lived here. My partner, Maxime, is a baker and so we decided to open Janine, a bakery-brewery focused on circular economy.

Our philosophy is to use the waste of one product, the bread, to create another product, beer. But our beer doesn't taste like bread.

Every day about 15-20 % of the bread we produce remains unsold, from these products we recover malts and yeasts.

Why did you decide to join the Co-Hop project?

It was hard to open a brewery on your own. We met the guys of DrinkThatBeer who introduced us to Thomas of Witloof. The cooperative model is a useful model to help and support each other by exchanging knowledge.

Why did you choose the name Janine?

It was my partner's grandmother's name. He has a wonderful memory of her as she went to get bread from the baker. We gave her name to our project in tribute to her.

Did you think about moving the bakery here to Co-Hop?

It was a hypothesis. But as a bakery we had set ourselves as a goal of having a place in a visible spot. For that reason, we stayed in the Albert area in Forest. At the bakery, you can buy Janine's beers.

You are one of the few women brewers in Brussels, how do you feel about it?

It's exciting to be one of the few. I hope more will come. I do not feel put aside, I have been well received and I feel very well with my colleagues. Beer is a good environment.

What kind of beers do you produce?

Janine's range counts six beers. The Rock N'Carol (an American pale ale), the Tromp L'Oeil, (a pale ale with ginger), the Ka Sa' Ye' (a New England IPA), the Max Attack, (a porter), the Super Smasch Bread, (a single hop single malt made by English ingredients) and the Volva Kveik, (a Kveik IPA).

I prefer to focus on new wave styles, not on traditional Belgian styles.

How do you think the Brussels beer scene will evolve in the coming years?

I think there's still room for other projects, especially for those who focus on different styles such as the Mule that makes German style beers. The scene is becoming more and more dynamic and different. Diversification is important. Maybe there will be some competition in the future, but that's not the case for now.

What is your favourite beer from Janine?

The Volva Kveik

What is your favourite beer from another Brussels brewery?

The Fugushima by Fugu Brewing Company.

Tipsy Tribe
Brewery&Distillery

Chau. de Jette 374, 1081 Koekelberg

Tipsy Tribe is the most recent brewery to arrive on the Brussels beer scene. To be precise it is a "Brewstillery" because in addition to the beer, they produce vodka, gin, whiskey and raki.

The founders are a very close-knit couple, Daniel the brewer, Belgian-American, and Aylin who deals with administration and marketing, Belgian-Turkish.

They are the first brewery to open in the so far from the beer point of view "arid" municipality of Koekelberg.

When I contacted them and went to visit the brewery, they were quite surprised by my interest. In fact, their brewery-distillery is still at the beginning.

Daniel and Aylin represent the new spirit that characterises the new Brussels breweries of the early twenties of this century; multicultural and innovative.

Sipping their delicious vodka, at 2pm, I had a very interesting chat with them.

Interview with Aylin and Daniel Fastenau:

How and when did your adventure begin?

Daniel: I worked as an AI consultant while Aylin worked as a communications consultant. At a certain moment, we decided to change our lives and embark on this wonderful adventure.

Like many, I started making beer at home with friends in 2016. We mostly did IPAs. At the time, it was difficult to find good IPAs in Brussels. It's a style that I like very much. In the USA where I came from, I tasted some delicious IPAs.

How did you choose this location?

Aylin: We've been looking for a location for three years, both in Brussels and outside Brussels. It was very complicated. We found this place at the beginning of 2021.

From what we know, this was a warehouse in the last century. At the beginning of the 2000s, it was rented by an evangelical church community, who in fact transformed it into a church. When the evangelicals abandoned it, it was occupied by a group of people who installed a kind of marijuana plantation. For obvious reasons, they weren't connected to the electric grid and they stole it from the neighbours. Their "project" ended quite badly as this abusive connection caused a fire that almost completely destroyed the roof.

When we took possession of the place, we found it in simply disastrous conditions; windows were broken, there was no gas, water or electricity, we found dead rats. It was raining inside.

We have worked hard to bring this place to a decent state.

Due to Covid the work was slow. In fact, we had wanted to open several months earlier.

Today, however, the building is in excellent condition; we have installed all the brewing equipment and also solar panels on the roof.

Will you have also a tap room?

Daniel: There's not enough room to set up a tap room. We will organise tastings. We also have a small garden where we will put some tables. In the garden, we are also growing our hops that will be used for special edition beers.

What kind of beers and spirits do you produce?

Daniel: I am working on different recipes: the Hipster Revenge, a double dry-hopped Belgian American IPA, the Chaotique, an American IPA, the Koekelbeer, a Belgian pale ale inspired by the municipality of Koekelberg, the Kicho, a Japanese IPA, the Clown Show, a DDH IPA and Summer Triple, which is nothing more than a Triple revisited and with an alcohol content lower than typical of that style.

We have also prepared a Vodka, the Vivre, made exclusively from Belgian cereals.

In the future, we will also produce Gin (launched in 2022), Raki (Aylin has Turkish origin) and Whisky (barrelled in March 2023).

We want to produce classic Belgian styles revisited; combining traditional elements with innovative elements inspired by our international background.

We aim to explore the frontiers of beer. We'll make combinations of the beers and the distillates we produce. We are going to try to use the yeasts of the spirits to make the beers, or the plants that we will use for gin to flavour our beers.

How do you think the Brussels beer scene will evolve in the coming years?

Daniel: I don't think the market is saturated yet. In the past, there were hundreds of breweries in Brussels.

In addition, nowadays, almost everywhere there is a trend that leads people to favour local products, of their own city, if not of their own neighbourhood. And I think this is starting to apply to breweries as well.

Of course, from an administrative point of view, opening a brewery is very complicated. Then to obtain permission for distillation is even more so.

Aylin: Opening a brewery in Belgium is always a challenge. Belgian beers have a mythical aura, but the movement of craft beers in Belgium is behind countries such as the USA, or the UK. So, I think there's still room. The important thing is to be original and offer new products.

What is your favourite beer from Tipsy Tribe?

Daniel: It is a question that is difficult to answer, much depends on the context, the moment and the company. I have high expectations about a beer that is not yet on sale, our Blanche.

Aylin: It's the same for me, too.

What is your favourite beer from another Brussels brewery?

Daniel: The Soleil of the Ermitage.

Aylin: The Mamouche of Cantillon.

Oskare

Allée Verte 52, 1000 Brussels

Oskare is a French brewery whose headquarters are located in Paris. In March 2022 they opened a second site in Brussels, near Arkose Canal, an indoor climbing gym.

The place is managed by an Italian of Venetian origin, Manuel Moretto. It presents itself as a welcoming and warm place with minimal decor and a beautiful rooftop. Beers are brewed on site in a small plant. It is the first foreign brewery to be established in Brussels to produce its own beers.

In the bar, located at the entrance, climbers quench their thirst. In addition to the beers produced on site, they offer on tap also beers from other Brussels breweries.

To understand how to combine climbing and brewing, I met their brewer: Felix.

Interview with Felix Bourée:

How and when did Oskare adventure begin in Brussels?

The project was born as part of Arkose, an indoor climbing gym chain born in France in 2018. Those who climb love to drink beer after their activity, and therefore we launched the idea of opening a microbrewery on site. In 2019, the Paris site opened, in 2021 the Brussels site opened.

A French brewery in Belgium, is that not a complicated challenge?

It's definitely a challenge. We want to show that we can do it by trying to offer different products. At the moment, we produce and sell only on site. In the future, we will probably start bottling and selling outside.

What kind of beers do you produce?

The beers all carry names related to climbing. The recipes were created by Loulu, the brewer of the Paris brewery. Here, we use the same recipes but we reinterpret them.

At the moment, we have four beers; the Boule (a smoked porter), the Pincette (an IPA), the Nofoot (a triple), the Sticky Chai, (a blanche). We'll have a pils soon.

What kind of customers do you have?

Lovers of climbing. They usually don't like to go too far in terms of styles. I try to make my customers taste different beers, but clearly we don't have an audience of beer geeks.

And what's about you, how and when did your adventure as a brewer begin?

I travelled a lot and discovered many beers. I started brewing with a friend and was enlightened by visiting a brewery in the Morvan Region of France. I did several internships, the first in Oskare in Paris, and then in several breweries in France. Then they entrusted me with the Brussels project.

How do you think the Brussels beer scene will evolve in the coming years?

I think there is still room for growth and space for everyone. In Paris, the beer scene has literally exploded. There are a lot of people who still don't know craft beers.

You have to bet on them, it is the market segment that can make a difference.

What is your favourite beer from Oskare?

The Boule, despite being smoked, is very drinkable.

What is your favourite beer from another Brussels brewery?

I really like the products of La Source and L'Ermitage. I can't choose.

Brasserie Taymans
Brouwerij

Rue Van Bortonne 46, 1090 Jette

The Brasserie Taymans is one of the most recent to arrive on the Brussels scene, and is the first brewery to open in the municipality of Jette.

This is an example of an old brewery brought back to life. The owners are six brothers, grandchildren of the last brewer, Pierre Taymans, who closed the brewery in 1970 when he retired.

The original brewery was called Brasserie-Malterie-Taymans and arose from collaboration between Adolphe-Philippe Taymans, a brewer from Molenbeek, and his father-in-law Pierre Belien, a beer merchant of Jette-Saint Pierre.

Like many breweries of the time, the beer of the house was the Lambic. The original location is not far from the current location on the site of the current Parc Garcet.

The brewery has an on-site plant of 10 hectolitres. At the moment, they produce the 1906, an IPA, whose name is dedicated to the year of construction of the old Brasserie warehouse and a saison.

The next beers will be their own lambic.

Part of the brewery's profits are donated to the Fondation Roi Baudouin to support cultural projects for young people.

The brewery is still in the first phase and so little more information is available.

Arever Belgian Craft Beer

Rue Frans Pepermans, 72, Evere

The work of mapping all the breweries that were established, or are being established, in Brussels was not easy.

Just before publishing the book I discovered the existence of a (micro) brewery that seems to be active since March 2017 in the municipality of Evere.

The name is dedicated to the handicrafts of Evere, the labels recall the symbol of the municipality and to Saint Vincent.

They have a very limited production (500 litres) and they produce directly at home.

In their range, there are four beers; an amber, an IPA, a double IPA and a double amber.

They also produced a Christmas beer and a chicory beer.

Gypsy Brewers and Beer Firms

In order to properly assess a beer scene, it is not only necessary to have a look to the presence of bars or breweries but also all the other efforts in this world.

I believe that for a brewery to be defined as a 'Brussels brewery' it must have its own centre of activities, and therefore the total or a partial share of its production, in Brussels. Nonetheless, there are other types of actors who by necessity, or due to lack of means, or pure choice are active in Brussels, and who do not brew their beer in the city.

For this reason, I decided to give some space in this book to those craft beer producers strongly gravitating towards Brussels, but who have not yet established production in the city. Gypsy brewers and beer firms are increasingly important players in Brussels. This may not please some purists, but I wish to present as complete a picture as possible.

To do that, I have selected six examples. I opted for six different projects managed by Brussels players which will have different destinies;

(i)   three breweries that are about to open their own production sites in the territory of Brussels,

(ii)   a brewery that, despite having a tap room in Brussels, has no intention of transferring its production to the city,

| (iii) | a brewery that due to external factors does not yet have its own production site (and probably won't have it in the city) |
| (iv) | a beer firm that has made the promotion of Brussels neighbourhoods its mission but which is still far from opening a site to produce beers independently. |

In the second part of this chapter, I will mention other projects that have their own range of activities in the city, or that produce in some city breweries. Given the difficulty in tracing this varied world, it is possible that I have forgotten to mention someone. In that case, I apologise for that. I will update this chapter in a future edition.

Brasserie Vandekelder

Among the most interesting examples of breweries that will soon open their own production site in Brussels is undoubtedly the Brasserie Vandekelder.

It was founded by nine friends and it is the only Brussels brewery with a Dutch-speaking majority. Their headquarters, in the municipality of Jette, is open for sale every third Saturday of the month. Their philosophy is "back to beer": they use only the four classic ingredients of beer (water, malt, hops and yeast) to create their own products.

One special feature is the recommendation to drink all their beers at a temperature of between 10 and 15 degrees Celsius.

To understand more about what is set to become a fully-fledged Brussels brewery, I had a chat with one of the nine founders, Bart Van Leemput.

Interview with Bart Van Leemput:

How and when did your adventure begin?

We started in 2016 in my cellar. We brewed a couple of times a month for a total of 60-90 litres. The name comes from where we started; Vandekelder, which in Flemish means "from the cellar".

In 2019, we felt that three of our recipes were ready for commercialisation. At the time there were many beer firms and gypsy brewers, it wasn't easy to find a place to brew. Our first beer was released just as Covid erupted in

Italy with the finding of Covid "patient one" in Italy in February 2020.

We had 2000 litres of beer ready and we didn't know what to do due to the lockdown closures. But thanks to the lockdown itself, people, forced into their houses, began to want to taste something different, and so we managed to sell everything in a month and a half.

Where do you make your beers?

We're still gypsy brewers. We currently work with the Annexe in Brussels, BeerSelect e't Hofbrouwerijke.

We have a small plant here on site that we use for experiments. We do tests every two weeks or so and when we are satisfied with the result we go to one of our partner breweries to do the crush. The goal, however, is to have a brewery of our own, here in Jette, by the end of 2023.

What kind of beers do you produce?

Our philosophy is "back to beer": we want to make beer with classic ingredients such as hops, grains etc. without using spices or other particular ingredients. We don't want to create anything "special". We have a different approach than most other breweries.

Our range currently counts seven beers; a pilsner, a Berliner Weisse, a barley wine, a "Belgian" IPA, an imperial stout, a black saison and a cuvée. In the future also an oud bruin.

Do you think participating in a beer festival is an added value?

We participate in beer festivals for fun and to meet new people. It is helpful to receive feedback on your beers, especially the most recent ones.

But you don't earn anything, if it's okay you match the costs.

It's interesting if you participate in beer festivals in your area, so potentially you can have a return of customers.

For a country of great beer tradition like Belgium is it possible to combine tradition with the innovations brought by craft breweries?

Belgium is a country of great beer tradition but each area has its own peculiarity. There's more openness than it seems. Styles like IPAs are working because people like them. Stout and barley wine work as well.

In addition, in Brussels there is an international community who is more open to novelties.

The role of the brewer is essential, he must explain to the customer the particularities of his product.

How do you think the Brussels beer scene will evolve in the coming years?

The beer scene in Brussels is exploding. In Antwerp and Ghent the situation is less lively as regards the new openings.

I think there's still room for other actors. The largest market in Brussels is for industrial beers, AB INBEV. It is necessary to encroach on that market and to promote craft beers to attract more customers. The majority of the bars have industrial beers on tap.

New actors in the craft beers world don't damage other craft beer actors, at least not for now.

What is your favourite beer from Vandekelder?

Each of us has a different idea. I really like Black Saison and Barley Wine.

What is your favourite beer from another Brussels brewery?

The Saison by L'Annexe.

Fugu Brewing Co.

Fugu Brewing's story represents the story of many actors in this world.

Fugu Brewing came into being thanks to a competition organised by a brewery open to amateur brewers, and the confidence gained from the good result achieved.

Like many others in the craft beer world, they do not yet have the resources to open their own site in Brussels, and therefore they survive by trying to earn space between beer shops and bars focused on craft beers.

In the coming years, we will probably not see Fugu Brewing among the Brussels breweries, but in another location. But their experience is emblematic of what is happening in this city.

I discussed this with one of the two founders, Samuel Lange, in their office/storage in Uccle.

Interview with Samuel Lange:

How and when did your adventure begin?

We've known each other since we were 18, and we both come from the province of Liège. In 2019, with Nico we went to the Dynamo Bar. For the first time, I tasted a craft beer, a beer by Northern Monk. I really liked it. From that moment, I began to taste everything and, later, I tried to replicate them. Every week we brewed a new beer. Especially IPA and its variations.

In 2020, we participated in a contest launched by the Brussels Beer Project; the Delta IPA Homebrewing

Competition. They made the Delta IPA recipe available and challenged the homebrewers to replicate it by sending them a sample.

With our two products, we arrived third and seventh. This gave us confidence and we decided to work hard on what then became our first beer, Fugushima, which we brewed and re-brewed many times until we thought it was ready. After that, we made it to taste in different places. Nico, in the meantime, took a course to become a brewer.

Where does the name "Fugu" come from?

Fugu is a typical dish of Japanese cuisine, based on ballfish, a fish that possesses within its organs a lethal dose of tetrodotoxin, edible only following appropriate preparation. It is necessary to do that to render harmless the poison and prevent it from contaminating the dish.

We chose this name one evening when, after several beers, we saw a video about this dish. Immediately, we compared it with beer production, which with an infection, may not come out well. That's how we chose Fugu.

Where do you make your beers? Are you planning to open a brewery in Brussels?

We make our batches at Anders brewery. Here where we are now, it is our store and also the place where we create our recipes.

In the future, the goal is to have our own brewery, but the COVID crisis and the rise in energy and raw material prices are delaying our project. Ideally, we would like to have a brewery in the triangle between Brussels, Namur and Liège. In the meantime, we will launch soon the "Fugu on tour" project.

At the moment, it is possible to find our beers in different craft beer shops in Brussels and in Belgium, and in some bars in Brussels and Liège. Our model is the brewpubs like La Source and Garage Beer in Barcelona and breweries like Northern Monk.

What kind of beers do you produce?

Mainly IPA and similar. Our flag product is Fugushima, a New England IPA. Then we have the Hop Circles (in version 1 and 2) which is a double IPA and the Tetrodaïne which is a hoppy lager.

How do you think the Brussels beer scene will evolve in the coming years?

I think people are going back to local products. They look a lot more at quality. That's why breweries are returning to Brussels.

I think, there is still a lot of space, especially in Brussels. Probably, it is more complex outside Brussels. However, there is a brewery like Misery that is having a lot of success. They are in the middle of the Ardennes region. Moreover, there are not many breweries focusing on IPAs in Belgium.

What is your favourite beer from Fugu Brewing?

The Hop Circles.

What is your favourite beer from another Brussels brewery?

The Meute of La Source.

Gasbeek Brewing Co.

Gansbeek Brewing is one of those breweries that, while referring to Brussels (the name recalls two different municipalities Gaanschoren and Etterbeek, where the two founders live, the Belgian Sébastien and the Spanish Luis), produces out of town and has no intention of moving in.

Their tap room is located in the old Hospice Pacheco, not far from Place Sainte Catherine. Today the project is called Grand Hospice and is in temporary occupation of the venue that hosts various cultural and commercial activities.

I met with Sébastien in order to try to understand more about their project.

Interview with Sébastien Cantineau:

How and when did your adventure begin?

I started in 2017 as a homebrewer. My partner, Luis, joined later. We produced beer at home for a couple of years. After that we considered ourselves sufficiently satisfied with the results, we decided to try to make the big leap.

We found the De Meesteer microbrewery, and they were available to host us. The only condition that the brewer imposed on us was that we had to deal exclusively with our brews. He trained us, and advises us still today.

Currently, in the same location there is also the Brasserie Punaise. The goal is to purchase a brewery within a few years.

In Brussels or elsewhere?

Costs are very high in Brussels. Outside Brussels, there are facilities with excellent equipment at lower cost. Our focus is on Belgium, not just on Brussels.

What kind of beers do you produce?

We produce classic styles revisiting the aromas. The goal is to bring people who usually drink industrial beers, to drink craft beers focusing on well-known styles. The objective is to attract potential customers by offering a product that they already know. We use 100 % Belgian ingredients.

At the moment, our range consists of a pale ale, a blonde, a brown ale and a triple. Then we have two barrel aged beers that we are very proud of, and that are going very strong.

The first is the Triple Bourbon Barrel Aged. It is a triple aged for six months in Bourbon barrels of the Heaven Hill Distillery in Kentucky.

The second is the Triple Red Wine Barrel Aged, a triple aged for six months in Bordeaux barrels of the Domaine de Baronarques in Carcassonne, France.

A Rye Whisky Barrel Aged will be ready soon. And soon, we will produce a pils dedicated to the football team of my municipality, Gaanshoren.

How do you think the Brussels beer scene will evolve in the coming years?

I think that it's up to the brewer to create his own community. Brussels is bound to get to a point where every bar or almost will have its own beer, as in the past. Our aim is to create a community of customers.

What is your favourite beer from Gansbeek Brewing Co.?

The Triple Bourbon Barrel Aged.

What is your favourite beer from another Brussels brewery?

The Epervier IPA of La Source.

Bières de Quartiers

"In Belgium, you can do a lot of things with beer". This sentence by Gregoire, the founder of Bières de Quartiers, underlines very well the importance of beer for Brussels and for Belgium.

Bières de Quartiers is a project that goes beyond beer production. Each beer is dedicated to a particular neighbourhood of Brussels. Behind each recipe, there is research work on the history and characteristics of the neighbourhood. More importantly, Bières de Quartiers aims to create a relationship between neighbours, traders and actors in the neighbourhood itself. Not all of their beers are brewed in the city but it is undeniable that the project is tied to Brussels.

I met Gregoire in their temporary headquarters in an old print shop in the university district.

Interview with Gregoire Malcause:

How did your adventure begin?

The project was created by me and my partner Bruno. We are friends since childhood. We studied bio-engineering together, he continued while I turned to business. Bruno had long been creating recipes for beers, while I participated in many projects related to the development of the Brussels districts.

One day we talked about tying the two things together, creating new beers dedicated to neighbourhoods, and using beer to finance projects dedicated to the development of the neighbourhood.

The first experiment was a beer dedicated to the Trois Tilleuls district in Watermael-Boitsfort. We created a beer for Bruno's tennis sports club. We brewed one hundred litres that were soon consumed. Then, we continued with another neighbourhood of Watermael-Boitsfort and so on.

Our first objective is to develop a network between the different actors in a particular district. We try to bring around the table associations, with traders, cultural associations etc.. Often, when we do not have any contact on site, we contact the municipality, or the mayor himself to help us to make contact with as many local actors as possible.

We draft a small questionnaire in which we ask for particular stories related to the neighbourhood, or typical products of the place.

We try to create a product that is linked to the history of the neighbourhood, and that is reflected in the recipe or in the label. We want to encourage a sense of belonging to the neighbourhood, creating interactions. We see beer as a "trait d'union" of the community.

What is the logic behind your beers?

Each beer has a bicolour label in which the project is explained and there is written information about the neighbourhood. For each beer, there are eight different labels (four in French and four in Dutch), each one having a different piece of information. It's a kind of identity card of the neighbourhood.

When we launch a new beer, that beer is sold for a certain period only in the neighbourhood to which it is dedicated, usually in the local shops. At the beginning, the project was to allow availability only in their neighbourhood, but

145

it was financially unsustainable and almost impossible from a logistical point of view. In addition, people from other neighbourhoods wanted to buy them. So, after a certain amount of time these beers are also sold elsewhere.

We have eight permanent beers, each of one dedicated to a different neighbourhood, and obviously of a different style. In addition, we have several temporary beers. The idea is to be able to cover at least all the municipalities, but the core range will always remain the same or change only marginally.

It's not easy to communicate what's behind it. Many people buy our beers only for the name.

In some neighbourhoods, such as in the centre, a beer was sold exclusively by the Traders' Association and the Parents' Association with EUR 1 additional margin to finance their activities.

They create a link between consumers and traders in the neighbourhood. In Belgium, you can do a lot of things with beer.

Bières de Quartiers aims to bring people closer to craft beer by bringing them closer to their neighbourhood and to the people who live in their neighbourhood.

We have also created a festival called "Salukes Voisins". It is the first Brussels festival dedicated to projects in the neighbourhoods.

What kind of beers do you produce?

Different styles. For example, for the neighbourhood of Place Flagey we have a lager. This is the HoReCa district par excellence and so we wanted a beer that is easy to drink. Also nearby, there was the Brasserie d'Ixelles that produced the Ixelles Helles.

Then we have the Wiener, (a spicy saison), the Trois Tilleus (a blonde), the Chasseurs Ardennais which is an Amber Smoked Ale, the Stockel, (a hoppy saison), the Saint Boniface, (a blanche), the Schweitzer, which is a Golden Ale, the CimDix which is a White IPA, the Uccle Centre which is a red IPA, the Parvis that is a blonde ale, La Cinquantenaire which is a pale ale and the Plateau Avijl which is a dubbel.

In which breweries do you produce your beers?

At Valduc, Jandrain-Jandrenuollie, Renard and Binchoise outside Brussels. At En Stomelings and Co-Hop in Brussels. At Co-Hop, we make our temporary beers in cans. We tried to brew only in Brussels but it was not possible.

Do you plan to open your own brewery?

Yes, we would love it and we have talked about that. It would be ideal also to use it as headquarters to bring together the various actors of the neighbourhoods with which we work. But for now it's just an idea.

How do you think the Brussels beer scene will evolve in the coming years?

Craft breweries still have room for expansion. Covid hit everyone hard, but sales of industrial breweries dropped more than those of the craft breweries. People are more sensitive to local products and more attentive to tastes, and this facilitates craft products in general.

The brewpub model is the one that works the most. Breweries without a tap room are enduring a bad period. Every brewery must take into account that beer lovers more and more often like to change, and therefore those who have many recipes can better cover this demand.

What is your favourite beer from Bières de Quartiers?

Usually, the last one that we launch. I love to change depending on the day, or the season, or the mood. If I have to pick one, I opt for the Chasseurs Ardennais, an Amber Smoked Ale.

What is your favourite beer from another Brussels brewery?

The Black Saison by L'Annexe.

Bières Artisanales Waterghem

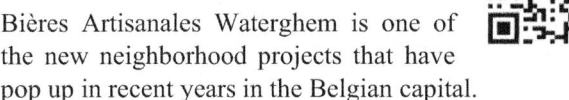

Bières Artisanales Waterghem is one of the new neighborhood projects that have pop up in recent years in the Belgian capital.

The name recalls the two Brussels municipalities of Watermael-Boitsfort and Auderghem. It is a family project, literally born in the home of its creator.

Gauthier, the brewer, received me at his beautiful home in the municipality of Auderghem where, tasting his Saison (Halvenalf), he explained me the origins and aspirations of this small but interesting beer project.

Interview with Gauthier Crèvecoeur:

How and when did your adventure begin?

The idea came to me about ten years ago. I always loved beers, however I was not satisfied with the products available on the market.

Once, I met a group of homebrewers with whom I started brewing beer. Later, I continued by my own. The first results were not encouraging but slowly I improved.

I read a lot of different forums about homebrewing and studied many books. I tried to brew several recipes. Over time, my products were appreciated by friends and neighbours and so I decided to make it a profession.

I started brewing at Brasserie Valduc. I got along well because they are very competent and nice people. However, they brewed my beers for me and I dind't like it. I felt disconnected from my products.

We received our first cases and kegs just a few days before the outbreak of the Covid pandemic. A disaster since we had to consume all the beers ourselves.

After the pandemic, we started to sell it to bars and restaurants. However, we found a lot of difficulty.

So, we decided to change and started brewing at Brasserie Artisanale et Didactique du Flo in Wallonia. This brewery offers the possibility to brew your own beer on site. I regained the "contact with beer" I had lost and improved a lot thanks to their advices.

We make five to six batch a year for each of our beers. My wife helps me in the project. The idea in the short term is to increase production to 1000 liters annually.

What kind of beers do you produce?

Currently, we have four beers in our range. Bis Repetita, our first creation, is a Belgian Pale Ale. Then we have Marquise (Session IPA), Halvenalf (Saison) and the latest addition, Rivale, a hoppy Blanche.

They can be found for sale in restaurants and neighborhood stores here in Auderghem and Watermael-Boisfort. They will soon be available in other parts of the city.

Do you have a plan to open your own brewery?

Yes, I do. It is a medium/long-term project. At the moment, there are not the right conditions. We would like to have a brewery or a brewpub with the possibility to cook and eat onsite.

We want to keep it small so that we never lose the link with our products. The idea is to open here in Auderghem, where there used to be several breweries and now there are none left.

How do you think the Brussels beer scene will evolve in the coming years?

There is still room for additional breweries. Before, there were many breweries in Brussels. Then, the big industrial groups took over and destroyed the market, but little by little some small realities are re-emerging.

I dream of a city full of many breweries producing many different styles. In the wine regions of France, there are plenty of family wineries that produce and sell their wine directly or in local restaurants or shops. I hope the same thing could happen here.

What is your model as a brewery?

I really appreciate Brasserie de la Senne. They started from nothing and created a model that allowed their beers to make their way into bars, restaurants and neighbourhood shops. They produce very good beers. I also like Brasserie De Ranke and their products.

What is your favourite beer from Bières Artisanales Waterghem?

Bis Repetita, the first beer that I brewed.

What is your favourite beer from another Brussels brewery?

Zenne Pils, preferably on tap.

Forest Brewing

Forest Brewing is one of the most interesting projects emerging on the Brussels beer scene.

Created by Michaël Boutriaux (author of the board game **The Belgian Beers Race Dice**), Cédric Gheenens and Antoine Pierson (founder and owner of the Beershop "Malt Attacks" in St.Gilles) it focuses on the production of fruity sours and dark beers. Their aim is to open a brewpub in the municipality of Forest in the coming years. To find out more about their project, I had a chat with Michaël Boutriaux.

Interview with Michaël Boutriaux:

How and when did your adventure begin?

The project was born in 2023 on the initiative of myself and some friends and neighbours like Cedric and Antoine from Malt Attacks. We have always been passionate about beer.

We brew in a small homebrewery and serve our beers mainly among friends and at private parties. Joel, brewer at Brasserie de la Mule, gives us lots of advice.

What kind of beers do you produce?

We are navigating between fruity sour and black beers. As sours we have Aux (a sour with a lot of fruit variation), the Love Philter (Sour Milkshake Raspberry) and the Ladanas (Pineapple White beer)

As black beers the Sup porter (Dry Hopped Porter), the Brutomium (Stout) and the Sour de Porc (Stou).

In our range we have also a bunch of classical (saison, blonde, IPA).

Do you have a plan to open your own brewery?

Yes. The idea is to open a brewpub here in Forest. But not now, the market does not offer the right conditions. We will do it in the next years.

How do you think the Brussels beer scene will evolve in the coming years?

There are many ideas and many projects but the economic situation is not ideal. There are several breweries that are in trouble. I think the model for the future is the brewpub. Brewing beer and selling it directly to your customers, creating a sense of community in your area. Like it was in the past.

What is your favourite beer from Forest Brewing?

The Cassandric, the "ultra" Raspberry version of our Love Philter.

What is your favourite beer from another Brussels brewery?

Berliner Weisse by Brasserie de la Mule.

Other projects

Visiting the different bars and the beer shops of Brussels, you will come across other beers of breweries operating in Brussels. Here is a non-exhaustive list.

The best known and easiest to find is probably **Brewksel**, active since 2016 and with active participation in several local beer festivals. They produce new wave beers and have created a very special beer with Brussels sprouts.

Then there is **Wonder Bru**, founded in 2022 and which aims to open a hop farm in the surroundings of Brussels. For now, they produce only one beer, Mate Brew, which, as its name suggests, is infused with the famous Argentine drink. They produce it at Co-Hop.

There is also a series of projects that produce their own beers at L'Annexe: **Alpha Spika**, **Don Dub Craft Beers** and **La Flaque**.

Also in L'Annexe **La Biche** is produced, a "solidarity" beer born from a project launched in 2020, in the midst of the Covid pandemic, to support the increasing number of homeless people that crowded Parvis of St. Gilles. The profits of the sale of this beer go to the Association L'Entraide de Saint-Gilles", which supports the homeless.

In the Chatelain area you can find the new beers of **Plaisir.beer**, a new beer firm that produces at the Brasserie Didactique du Flo in Hannut. Also, **Brussels Hoppist** beers are produced at Brasserie du Flo.

In the Sablon area, you can find **Zoevel (Be Tasty)**, a beer brewed in collaboration with Brasserie de la Lesse and dedicated to Sablon.

Also worth trying is **Flow**, a beer produced in a micro plant for the Food Market Wolf, a few steps from the Grand Place.

Another interesting novwelty is the project **FLORA** who aims to brew with flowers.

In 2023, the **Brasserie H20** will resume operations in Brussels. They have started collaboration with the Moeder Lambic Fontanas, which will become a brewpub.

And then Alexis from Brasserie En Stomelings just launched **OSMA**, a barrel aged beer project.

In July 2024, En Stomelings handed over equipment to **Amère à boire** and **L'Impasse** cafés. They will brew their own beers and offered them on taps in their cafés.

Even Brussels' Dutch-speaking university Vrije Universiteit Brussel (VUB) has invested €3 million to start brewing beer (and baking bread and making chocolate) on its Etterbeek campus.

Finally, another interesting project; **Bobby Brewery**, a brewery located in the municipality of Ittre, produces Lambic at the Den Herberg brewery in Halle and will allow for fermentation in barrels in the cellars of the Halles de St.Géry for a year and a half. The product was unveiled in early November 2022 and is available at the historic (but renovated) Greenwich Bar in the city centre.

Brussels district by district

In this second part of this book, we visit the different neighbourhoods of Brussels. For each neighbourhood, you will find a dedicated chapter.

At the beginning of each chapter, I provide a map with the places that I suggest. Each chapter is divided into two parts. In the first part, you will find a "suggested beer tour" with the best places to taste craft beers. In the second part, you will find other good places to visit.

In each chapter, I have added also some historical and cultural references related to the places you visit.

With regard to the selection, I used a mix of objective criteria such as the quality of the "beer menu", the prices, and the service. Every judgment on the premises is purely subjective, dictated by my tastes and my experience over more than ten years of life in Brussels.

For each place that I mention, I have indicated the number of beers available (On tap and in bottle) as well as the possibility to eat. Keep in mind that these elements may will be different at the moment of the purchase of this book.

Another aspect to also keep in mind is that in Brussels beer is everywhere. But in the majority of cases you will find industrial beers (even in several of the aforementioned premises). Unfortunately, even in Brussels you can count the number of proper craft beer bars on the fingers of your hand.

Have a tasty trip and have fun!

University District — ULB

The Solbosch district of the ULB is more commonly called the University District or "Cimitiere d'Ixelles", due to the presence of one of the most important historical cemeteries in the city.

It is one of the places that I love the most. I lived there for many years; first for my Erasmus program and then for the Master's degree, both at the Université Libre de Bruxelles (Free University of Brussels in English).

The Cimitiere d'Ixelles is one of the largest cemeteries in Belgium and hosts remarkable monuments. There is the tomb of the famous Brussels architect Victor Horta, who also designed the sumptuous mausoleum of the Solvay family. The cemetery also contains another wonderful sculpture; the tomb in "blue stone" by Charles de Coster with a statue of Thijl Uylenspiegel.

Due to the presence of military tombs (including that of the famous General of the French Revolution Georges Boulanger) there are also several historical testimonies. There are also the tombs of several artists and intellectuals such as Jules Bordet, Baron Empain, Eugène Ysa, Camille Lemonnier, the inventor of the famous chocolate praline Frédéric Neuhaus, and the founder of the Lazio football team, Luigi Bigiarelli.

Despite the gloomy atmosphere of the cemetery, in the neighbourhood there is a kind of "Gothic" atmosphere with many parties, bars with music and full with people. There is always someone in the street, the average age is quite low as it is a neighbourhood inhabited by a large community of students. The area is located between Campus Solbosch and Campus La Plaine of the Free University of Brussels with many university residences and student kots.

To get there, you must take the famous bus number 71 of the STIB. Anyone who has studied in Brussels, at ULB or Flemish sister VUB knows this important line from the Delta terminus (where there is a hospital and a train station) to De Brouckere in the heart of the city. The neighbourhood lends itself to that practice commonly known as "pub crawling".

At the 71-line bus stop "Cimitiere d'Ixelles", you go straight into the heart of the nightlife along the local section of the Chaussee de Boondael. On the left, you will find, behind an old metal gate, the famous **Tavernier**, the kingdom of many crazy university evenings. Here, order a Duvel Verte (7 %, pleasantly bitter and difficult to find in other places). The party atmosphere will surely lead you to make another order (choose a great St. Feuillien Blonde).

After the Tavernier, continue to follow the Chaussee de Boondael, at the corner with the Avenue des Saisons you will find **Le Gauguin**. It is a classic Belgian bistro with wooden interiors where you can order a good Westmalle Triple.

Continue to follow the Chausse de Boondael to Place de la Petite Suisse. Here, you should stop at **Le**

Montmartre, an authentic institution of the neighbourhood with always a fresh Saison Dupont on tap and a pool table for exiting challenges between friends. It is not easy to stop drinking a Saison Dupont on tap, but, your tour is not yet finished. Turn left and go to Rue Elise, where you will find one of the jewels of this very interesting neighbourhood: the **Atelier de la Soif**[10].

The Atelier de la soif is the heir to the historic bar L'Atelier that since 1977 had become a reference point for beer enthusiasts and students in the area.

Like many other places, it failed due to the collapse of the business during the COVID pandemic. It reopened on the initiative of a new young owner in September 2021. It looks like an old garage, without windows and with the classic wooden interiors.

The menu of the beers, divided by style, is placed on a wooden panel hanging on the wall. To keep the right high amount of alcohol level, order a St. Bernardus 10, a Quadrupel from the homonymous brewery.

Now, you feel like a student. So, Why don't you order also a "Submarine"? (it's mixed with a Jupiler but you won't tell anyone).

It's time to get back. Retrace the path you have taken and make a refreshing stop at the Seven Days. With everything you've been drinking, you deserve a Mitrallette[11]!

---

[10] Unfortunately, it seems that this place has again closed.
[11] A mitraillette is a type of sandwich in Belgium commonly served at friteries and cafés. It is popular among students.

Returning to the roundabout of the Cimitiere d'Ixelles you can wait for the 71, the Noctis or take a taxi. But if you want one last drink, go to the Chaussee de Boondael, but this time on the left and stop at **Le Corto** along with the last heroes of the night.

Le Corto, dedicated to the homonymous protagonist of the comics' saga, is a small and welcoming neighbourhood bar that offers snacks during the day and at night turns into an authentic bar of the Antilles. Close with a Jambe de Bois from Brasserie de la Senne and then go to sleep!

To not miss:

Le Tavernier

Chaussée de Boondael 445-1050 Ixelles
Mon — Sat 11-02 Sun 14-01
11 taps, 30+ bottled beers, snacks, live music.

Le Montmartre

Chau. de Boondael 344, 1050 Ixelles
Mon — Fri 11-02 Sat — Sun 15-02
12 taps, 30+ bottled beers, snacks, live music

Le Gauguin

Chau. de Boondael 420, 1050 Ixelles
Mon — Sun 11-02
7 taps, 20+ bottled beers, snacks.

L'Atelier de la Soif

Rue Elise 77, 1050 Ixelles
Mon — Sun 18-01
8 taps, 60+ bottled beers, snacks.

Le Corto

Chau. de Boondael 485, 1050 Ixelles
Mon — Sun 16-02
3 taps, 20+ bottled beers, small restaurant.

Other suggestions:

La Bécasse

Chau. de Boondael 476, 1050 Ixelles
Mon — Sun 10-1.30
2 taps, 40+ bottled beers

Typical Belgian brasserie and authentic institution in the neighbourhood, La Bécasse offers a menu with all the classics of Belgian cuisine and a good list of beers and wines. In honour of the university district and its diverse population, it remains open until late.

Café Bastoche

Chau. de Boondael 473, 1050 Ixelles
Mon — Sun 11-01
6 taps, 10+ bottled beers
Commonly known as "Bastoche" is one of the most famous Brasseries in Ixelles having opened in 1927. After failing, it reopened in 2021.

Flagey

In the heart of the municipality of Ixelles, the Flagey district is a cosmopolitan crossroads as well as a real cultural hub.

The square was named in honour of Eugène Flagey, Mayor of Ixelles from 1935 to 1953. It was formerly called Place Sainte-Croix. It is one of the most important hubs in the city with ten streets converging on it. It is right beside Ixelles ponds which are surrounded by beautiful "maisons de maître". The square is well connected to the rest of the city by various bus lines and tram 81.

Under the square, a large tank was built for the control floods (necessary due to the low altitude of the ground and the high level of groundwater). There is also an underground parking lot. The area now covered by the square was covered by the ponds until 1860, when one of the original ponds was dried up as part of a new urban project.

The presence of ponds, from these parts improperly called "lakes", populated by ducks makes the atmosphere very idyllic by day and particularly on Sunday, when families and runners congregate in the area. But from happy hour time to late evening, Place Flagey is one of the hubs of Brussel's fun.

The narrow streets around the square offer several bars, restaurants and shops that liven the neighbourhood. On Saturdays and Sundays, there is a market, with a wide choice of stalls with fruit, vegetables, cheese and street food.

There is a prominent view the "Flagey building". Designed as a classic of Belgian culture, it is known as the 'paquebot jaune' (yellow boat) for its characteristic shape. It was built in the 1930s as a radio studio and recording complex.

But with the remarkable growth of the television industry, it became too small, and the television and radio studios were moved elsewhere. The Flagey building remained closed for some time, before being restructured to host several cultural initiatives.

Today, it hosts the Cinematek, a paradise for movie lovers, showing various classic and contemporary films. There are also concerts (jazz or classic music), literary meetings and workshops for children.

Due to a large Portuguese presence in the area, lusitanophiles will happily find various restaurants, bars and grocery stores with Portugese food, wine and goods.

From the beer point of view, the area is rich and very interesting.

Your beer tour can only start from the **Cafe Belga**, a large Art Deco café right on the ground floor of the Flagey building. It was previously a meeting place for artists and actors, but is now mostly frequented by young people. However, it remains an indispensable part of the Brussels bar scene, and loved by the locals. The interior is very spacious, but also rather noisy and confusing.

If the weather is good, take a seat at an outdoor table on one of the largest terraces in the city. Otherwise look for a place inside. To order a drink, you must go to the counter, but given its length, it is not easy to be served. Be patient. Order a La Cambre Blonde of the Abbaye de La Cambre. The Abbey is just 5-minute walk from the Café Belga (however, it is brewed in Mechelen by the Het Anker brewery).

From Café Belga, go towards the church and turn left into Rue du Belvedere. Your next stop is **Le Murmure**, another monolith of Flagey's brewery scene.

Le Murmure is something between a university bar and an old bohemian cafe. The majority of the customers are students from the nearby Faculty of Architecture of the ULB and artists. It is a fascinating place, a bit sloppy with the classic wooden interiors, the classic pool and a blackboard with the menu of the beers. Order a VanderGhinste Oud Bruin, as it is not easy to find this beer at such advantageous price.

A few metres further on, you will find another bar not to be missed for your tour: **L'amère à boire**, a very well-known and successful Brussels bar. They have opened two other locations with the same name in the Brussels municipalities of St. Gilles and Uccle (the latter near the Uccle-Calevoet train station). There is a menu with more than 150 beers and a very competent staff. It's time to get a great XX Bitter by De Ranke!

Most likely in the three previous bars you did not order only one beer per place. Therefore, you should be hungry. Place Flagey area offers several good restaurants with food from all over the world. To keep it simple, I recommend the classic "Frites" at the kiosk in the middle of the square. There is a diatribe in Brussels about which are the best frites between the kiosk in Place Flagey and the famous "Maison Antoine" in Place Jourdan. I will let you decide between the two. I suggest you to pair the "frites" with the sauce "poivre"... it's delicious and makes you thirsty, helping you to prepare for the last (?) stop of your tour among the best beer bars in Flagey: **Le Pantin**.

From the Frites kiosk, go towards the bus/tram stop and then turn right into Chaussee d'Ixelles. On the left, at number 355 you will find Le Pantin.

It is real gem, hidden from the eyes of the most. Le Pantin is one of the few bars left in Brussels where chess players continue to meet for timeless games. The atmosphere is very bohemian and there is a mixed clientele of students and locals. Several old board games are also available for customers. The upper floor is characterised by the presence of old armchairs, in which you can literally sink, and tables arranged in a causal way. It is the place with the ideal setting to close your evening by sipping a divine and timeless Avec les Bon Voeux of Brasserie Dupont and closing with a Chartreuse.

Do not miss:

Cafe Belga

PL. Eugène Flagey 18, 1050 Ixelles
Mon — Sun 08-02
10 taps, 30+ bottled beers, snacks.

Le Murmure

Rue du Belvédère 18, 1050 Ixelles
Mon — Sun 16-04
6 taps, 60+ bottled beers, snacks.

L'Amère à boire

Rue du Belvédère 8, 1050 Ixelles
Mon — Sun 16-02
12 taps, 150+ bottled beers, snacks.

Le Pantin

Chau. d'Ixelles 355, 1050 Ixelles
Mon — Sun 10-03
4 taps, 40+ bottled beers, snacks
Other suggestions:

De Valera's

PL. Eugène Flagey 17, 1050 Ixelles
Mon — Fri 17-02 Sat 11-02 Sun 11-01
9 taps, 25+ bottled beers, pub kitchen.

Located between the Place Flagey and the ponds of Ixelles, it is one of the best known Irish pubs in the city. Good choice of Belgian beers in addition to the familiar Irish beers. Classic pub cuisine and the possibility to watch sports on the many screens in the pub.

Bar du Marché

Rue Alphonse De Witte 12, 1050 Ixelles
Mon — Sun 17-02
4 taps, 10+ bottled beers, snacks.

Trendy place, very popular in the late evening. Here the cocktails are big, but among the bottled beers there is some local Brussels products.

The Melting Potes

Rue du Belvédère 16, 1050 Ixelles
Tue — Thu 17.30-02 Fri 17.30-03 Sat — Mon 17.30-00
Sun closed
5 taps, 70+ bottled beers, pizza&tapas

It is defined as a "sports bar" and broadcasts every variety
of sport through six maxi screens. Possibility to play pool
or darts. Large choice of beers.

The Black Sheep

Chau. de Boondael 8, 1050 Ixelles
Wed — Sun 17-02 Mon — Closed Sea
7 taps, 40+ bottled beers, catering.

Very nice gastropub with good choice of fish-based
dishes. Excellent choice of beers with the peculiarity of
having the Paix Dieu on tap.

Flip

Chau. de Boondael 40, 1050 Ixelles
Tue — Thu 17-01 Fri 17.30-03 Fri — Sat 17-02 Sun —
Mon closed
3 taps, 80+ bottled beers, snacks.

It is a small vintage bar close to L'Espace Lumen. On the
walls works by young artists are exhibited. Very eclectic
music, a magnificent Sabena memorabilia and good
choice of beer.

Malting Pot

See Beer store page 265.

Felix Bar Café

Rue Félix Bovie 48, 1050 Ixelles
Mon — Sun 08-23
5 taps, + 20 bottles, snacks.

Until 2020, it was a classic old neighbourhood cafe. The new management chose to renew it to attract younger customers. Very spacious terrace and good choice of beer.

La Brique de Flagey

Rue de la Brasserie 98A, 1050 Ixelles
Mon — Sun 10-01
7 taps, 40+ bottles
Last entry into the crowded Flagey area with its many local bars. Excellent choice of beers (with many Brussels beers) and excellent cocktails. It is possible, by ordering a drink, to sit down and enjoy the takeaway dishes of My Tannour, a very popular Syrian restaurant, located next door.

Place Fernand Cocq — Matongé — Quartier Saint Boniface

The Chaussee d'Ixelles offers a very interesting insight of the multiethnicity of Brussels.

Starting from the Place Flagey, you will immediately come across one of the many Portuguese neighbourhoods that were formed in the city in the last century due to a massive emigration from Portugal. Continuing along the street, you arrive at Place Fernand Cocq.

The square is dedicated to the lawyer Fernand Cocq, first a councillor and then mayor of the Municipality of Ixelles at the time of the First World War. He became famous as one of the most strenuous defenders of the French language in Belgium and of the role of Wallonia in the Kingdom of Belgium.

The square has been recently renovated and now presents as a beautiful square almost totally pedestrianised with trees and fountains, and with various bars and restaurants on the sides.

To the south of the square stands a building of important neoclassical style that hosts the Municipality.

Your tour starts at **Contrebande** on Place Fernand Cocq. It is a co-operative bar opened in 2016 in the premises of an old police station. It has two halls (one can be rented for events) and two terraces (one inside and the other external). It specialises in organic products and beers from small Belgian or micro-breweries. Here, I suggest you to order a fresh Super Sanglier from Brasserie Minne on tap and then warm up with a stunning Merevertus, the triple flagship of the very interesting Millevertus brewery, located in Belgian Luxembourg.

Leave the Contrebande behind and continue to Rue de la Tulipe, turn left into Rue Jules Bouillon and at the bottom of the right corner you will find **L'Athenée**.

Located behind the Church of Saint Boniface, it is a small bar with wooden interiors and walls covered with writings and graffiti of all kinds. The choice of beers is very interesting and the prices are very good. With good weather, the terrace of the bar extends to the surrounding space. Order a Saisonneke from Belgoo brewery and get ready for the next stop.

The Athenée geographically marks the beginning of the picturesque district of Matongé, the African quarter of Brussels.

Matongé came into being in 1960, the year in which the controversial Belgian colonial experience ended with the independence of Zaire, today the Democratic Republic of the Congo. It took its name from a neighbourhood in the capital of Kinshasa, known for being the centre of Congolese culture and music.

The first nucleus of Matongé arose thanks to the Belgian aristocrat Monique Van der Straten who founded the Maison Africaine (the Maisaf) in the late 1950s, a hostel that soon became a meeting place for the African diaspora.

In the 1990s, however, the neighbourhood was the scene of clashes and social tensions due to the level of delinquency that existed in its streets. For many years Matongé was considered as an off limits area.

Today, there is a definite improvement in the situation. The neighbourhood has become a lively, creative and attracts many young people with its ethnic restaurants, crowded bars, and numerous shops.

At the entrance of the neighbourhood, at the Porte de Namur metro stop, there is a beautiful mural with the words "Porte de Namur or Porte de l'amour?" and which portrays a typical scene of a party day in the neighbourhood; women who weave hair, bright colours, love...This represents the essence of a neighbourhood that has overcome most of its problems by creating a wonderful mélange of colours, languages, sounds and smells.

From L'Athenée, continue on Rue Bourrè then turn left onto Rue Lounge Vie and again left on Rue de la Paix. At number 31, you will find the **Zonneklop**, a typical party bar that fits perfectly in the atmosphere of the neighbourhood with its multi-ethnic clientele and its timeless evenings. Order one or more Zinnebir from Brasserie de la Senne and let yourself be carried away by the music and the atmosphere of this bar.

But your tour is not over yet. Continue on Rue de La Paix until you reach Place Saint Boniface, at the steps of the church of Saint Boniface, one of the first neo-Gothic buildings built in the city in the nineteenth century. You can eat one of the best Carbonades Flamande of the city, paired with an excellent Trappist beer, at **Le Clan des**

Belges. Then, order the last drink at the **L'Ultime Atome**, a Gulden Draak, that will help you sleep well.

Do not miss:

Contrebande

PL. Fernand Cocq 6, 1050 Ixelles
Tue — Sun 14-01 Mon closed
5 taps, 50+ bottled beers, small catering, organic food.

L'Athenée

Rue Jules Bouillon 2, 1050 Ixelles
Mon — Sun 10-01
5 taps, 40+ bottled beers, snacks.

Zonneklop

Rue de la Paix 31, 1050 Ixelles
Mon — Sun 17-02
4 taps, 30+ bottled beers, small catering.

The Clan des Belges

See restaurants page 279.

L'Ultime Atome

See restaurants page 279.

Other suggestions:

De Haus

Chau. d'Ixelles 183, 1050 Ixelles
Fri — Sat 17.30-03 Mon closed Sun — Tue — Thu 17.30-01

4 taps, 30+ bottled beers, small restaurant.

Bar dedicated to gin lovers in all its variants. Good choice of beers.

Le Cocq Brussels

PL. Fernand Cocq 12, 1050 Ixelles
4 taps, 10+ bottled beers, snacks.

Recently opened (2021) it is called "Frits-cocq" as it allows you to order the famous "frites". Limited but interesting choice of beers.

The Ilot Corse

Rue du Collège 22, 1050 Ixelles
Tue — Sat 18.30-23

Wine bar with typical Corsican products. They have craft beers from Corsica (Brasserie Pietra).

Café Lutgarde

Chau. de Waterloo 393, 1050 Ixelles
Wed – Sat 15-01 Sund 14-23 Mon – Tue closed
7 taps, x bottles, food.

Second city's taproom of the young Abbaye d'Aywiers brewery. Opened in 2023, excellent selection beers of 'Lutgarde' brand and microbreweries from Brussels and Belgium.

Les Brassins

See restaurants page 279.

Cafe Aux Sans Souci

Rue Sans Souci 80, 1050 Ixelles
Tue – Sat 08.30-22 Sun – Mon closed
6 taps, + 20 bottles.
Classic Brussels neighbourhood estaminet with a varied clientele. Good choice of beers and classic board games available.

Viaduc

Rue du Viaduc 43, 1050 Ixelles
Tue – Sat 17-00 Sun – Mon closed
5 taps, +20 bottles.

Historic neighbourhood bar (opened in 1860) with classic wooden interior. Ideal place to drink beers from the Roman brewery of Oudenaarde. It is also one of the few places in Brussels where the (mainly French) tradition of drinking a beer accompanied by a Picon bitter has survived.

Chatelain — Bailli

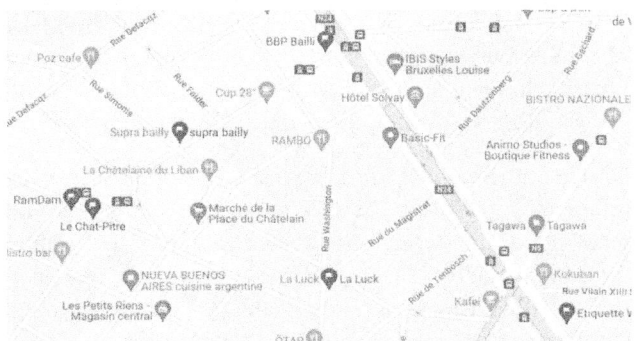

The Châtelain-Bailli district is a very popular residential district with its concept stores and colourful alleys with Art Nouveau facades.

Until the 1970s, it was a neighbourhood linked to the automotive industry. The centrepiece was the current Rue Américaine with the famous Maison d'Ieteren which over the years has hosted important brands such as Porsche, Audi and Volkswagen. In Rue Américaine, there is also Victor Horta's Maison Atelier.

Starting from the 1970s, low house prices began to attract many young people, because of the central location of the neighbourhood. A process of gentrification began peaking in the 1990s, when officials of the European Institutions began to settle in the neighbourhood. Property prices began to rise and many restaurants and boutiques opened.

On Wednesday, on the square of Châtelain there is a market with street food that runs until the evening when the square and its bars fill up for the happy hour.

The neighbourhood is bordered by the famous Avenue Louise, one of the city's most important arterial routes. The avenue extends from Place Louise to the Bois de la Cambre and is one of the most expensive in Brussels. There are numerous embassies, historical monuments and luxury clothing stores. The avenue owes its name to Princess Louise, the eldest daughter of King Leopold II.

During the Second World War, Avenue Louise became infamous for hosting the Gestapo offices where several members of the Belgian Resistance were tortured. Before the 1958 Universal Exhibition, it was completely renovated, and today is crossed, through an underground tunnel, by an urban highway called "Little Belt".

From the beer point of view, the Chatelain- Bailli district is not the best place in town. However, you can still find interesting places.

Your tour starts at **L'Etiquette**, located at number 326 of Avenue Louise. It is an elegant and very popular place for aperitifs and happy hour. The focus is on wines but has an excellent beer list. Order an Oude Gueuze of 3 Fonteinen.

Walk along Avenue Louise to the junction with Rue de Bailli. Just at the intersection it won't be hard to see the **Brussels Beer Project Bailli**, one of the three premises of the rampant Brussels brewery. The bar is on two floors and with a nice terrace-patio, it is always quite crowded. If you are lucky, you can find some guest brew, usually foreign, on tap. If not, opt for the Dark Sister, a Black IPA, in my opinion one of the best products among the many BBP beers.

Continue on Rue du Bailli until number 77. Your next stop is the **Supra Bailly**. For the people of the neighbourhood, it is a real institution being one of the few bars that hasn't suffered any form of gentrification. Order a St.Feuillen Blonde and go to the next stage.

Continue on Rue du Bailli and reach the Parvis de la Trinité. At the corner of the Rue de l'Aqueduc and the Rue du Tabellion, you will find the **Chat-Pitre**. Classic old neighbourhood bistro furnished with jazzmen statues and many beer cartons on which customers have drawn cats of all kinds. The venue is famous for being the meeting place for lovers of jazz music. Every Wednesday at 7 pm, there is a jazz concert followed by a jam session that often lasts until the early hours of the morning. It is a magical place for music lovers, where you can get on tiptoe, relax and enjoy the atmosphere. This is the classic place to order an excellent Orval.

A few meters from the Chat-Pitre, you will find without a doubt one of the most interesting places from the point of view of beer in the area; the **Clair/Obscur**, a place with a high-quality beer choice and the possibility to eat onsite.

To not miss:

Etiquette Wines

AV. Louise 326, 1050 Ixelles
Mon — Fri 12-00 Sat 18-00 Dom closed
30+ bottled beers, restaurant.

BBP Bailli

Rue du Bailli 1/A, 1000 Brussels
 Mon-Tue 17-00 Wed 17-01 Thu-Fri 17-02 Sat 15-02 Sun 15-00
30 taps, 20+ bottled beers, pizza.
Supra Bailli

Rue du Bailli 77, 1050 Ixelles
Mon — Sun 09-01
4 taps, 20+ bottled beers, snacks.

Chat-Pitre

Rue du Tabellion 1, 1050 Ixelles
Mon — Sun 17-05
2 taps, 10+ bottled beers, snacks.

Clair/Obscur

Rue de l'Aqueduc 61/63, 1060 Bruxelles
Mon – Wed 11.30 – 01 Thu – Fri 11.30 – 01, Sat 10.30 –
02 Sun 10.30 – 18
4 taps, +70 bottled beers, restaurant.

Other suggestions:

La Luck

Rue Washington 74, 1050 Ixelles
4 taps, 10+ bottled beers, restaurant.
Rising from the ashes of an English pub, the glorious The
Old Inn, is a rather fashionable brasserie. It has a limited
but interesting selection of beers from micro or small
breweries, on tap or bottled.

Kastar Cafe

Rue Lens 2, 1050 Ixelles
7 taps, 20+ bottles, snacks.
Modern reinterpretation of a classic neighbourhood bar.
Located close to Avenue Louise, it offers an interesting
choice of beers.

Bintje

Rue Simonis 62, 1050 Ixelles
Mon-Tue -Thu -Fri 18.30-22 Wed -Sat -Sun 12-22
10+ bottles, snacks.
The city's first "Bar à frites" with an interesting selection
of craft beers.

L'Impasse

Pl. du Châtelain 17, 1050 Ixelles
Mon – Thu 16 – 01 Fri – Sat 17 – 02 Sun 14 – 23
12 taps, 150+ bottled beers, snacks.
Very recent novelty. Same owners of L'Amère à Boire.

European Quarter

Brussels is the main seat of different Institutions of the European Union. It hosts the buildings of the European Commission, the Council, the European Parliament and various other bodies.

The "European Quarter" was formerly called Quartier Léopold, in honour of King Leopold I, who reigned over Belgium from 1831 to 1865. Until 1837, it was a normal neighbourhood of houses, farms and fields. Later, it was rezoned and some of the most influential personalities of the city and of all Belgium moved there. Parks were built, along with elegant palaces and libraries.

The situation further changed after the First World War, when nobles and bourgeois moved to the open countryside around the city. The old mansions were replaced by cold glass structures and the neighbourhood went over to office spaces. In 1957, there the first steps which led to what would become the European Union.

The neighbourhood has been in constant change, with continuous expropriations to make room for the institutions and the whole range of activities that revolves around them. Today, only a few buildings of the old Quartier Léopold still survive.

From the beer point of view, it is one of the busiest, and least Belgian, areas of the city. It offers many venues with the same beer offer. However, it is also possible to find good beers and visit interesting places. For this reason, I propose two different routes that will take you to the venues frequented by the Eurocracy and to the evergreen Irish pubs, and vice versa.

Place Luxembourg — Place de Londres

Start your tour from the famous Place Luxembourg. The nerve centre of the old Quartier Léopold, it was built in its current version between 1855 and 1861 in neoclassical and symmetrical style and just in front of the railway station, by the architect Antoine Trappeniers. The imperious building just in front of the place is the European Parliament.

In Place Luxembourg on Thursday evening, one of the most famous "after-work" aperitifs in the city is celebrated. You can have a Happy hour with industrial beer at half price until seven o'clock in the evening. The traffic is diverted due to the massive presence of jackets, ties and tailleur chatting and networking. Are you pluxing this evening? Or a simpler "Plux?" That's the most recurring phrase of Thursday throughout the European quarter.

The atmosphere is pleasant and festive but it is not easy to find good beers. I recommend entering the **Quartier Léopold** bar at number 9 of the square. It is the only bar in the city where you can enjoy a Pilsner Urquell properly tapped and honestly priced.

After Quartier Léopold cross the square, to the corner with Rue de Treves, go to **The Beer Factory**. It is well known brasserie of the area with excellent dishes and good choice of beer.

On site, you must order a Charles Quint blonde by the Het Anker brewery from Mechelen. They will serve it to you in a very special four-handle goblet. The legend says that Emperor Charles V of Habsburg, who was originally from the Belgian city of Ghent, went to a tavern to drink a beer. The waiter served a beer to him keeping it by the handle. The Emperor said to him, "How can I drink beer if you keep it by the handle?" Later the Emperor returned to the same tavern and asks for a beer. This time, it was served to him in a goblet with two handles. But again the waiter served it keeping it for the two handles. The Emperor reacted in the same way and the story repeated itself until it reached a 4-handle glass.

From Beer Factory, continue on Rue de Treves, turn left onto Rue du Trone and then right onto Chausse de Wavre. At number 176 you will find **Beer Mania**, which I personally consider one of the best places in Brussels to drink beer.

Opened in 1981, it was the first beer shop in the world to offer an online sales service in 1997. This kind of service continues today with the possibility to order beer and receive it in any corner of the globe. It offers its customers more than 500 types of beer, from almost all of the breweries in Belgium. It is equipped with two rooms and a beautiful terrace, and it is usually possible to taste beers on site and enjoy the classic "frites" or a rich plateau of cheeses. The owner, Michael Eftekhari, is one of the country's greatest beer connoisseurs. In addition, every beer is served in the glass for which it was created.

Order a Ter Dolen Triple or, if you are in a big group, a 0.75 bottle of Deus. You will definitely come back the next day to stock up with beers.

From Beer Mania, continue right on the Chaussee de Wavre for 200 meters, then turn left onto Rue Major Renè Dubreucq and walk to the Place de Londres, another of the more interesting places for a post-work drink.

Your first stop in the square will be **Au Stomelings**[12], one of the few authentic Brussels bars that survived in the area. It is a classic Belgian estaminet with wooden interiors and a terrace on the square for when there is good weather, a small counter and a delicious choice of beers. Order a Rochefort Trappist 10 and head across the square where, on the corner of Rue de Londres and Rue de Dublin you will find the **London Calling**, an ideal place to close the evening with various Brusseleir and live music.

Do not miss:

Quartier Léopold

Pl. du Luxembourg 9, 1050 Ixelles
Mon — Fri 12.30-22.30 Sat — Sun closed
6 taps, 10+ bottled beers, snacks.

The Beer Factory

Pl. du Luxembourg 6, 1050 Ixelles
Mon — Sat 11-23 Dom closed
8 taps, 10+ bottled beers, restaurant.

---

[12] At the moment, it is closed for renovations.

Beer Mania

Chau. de Wavre 174/176, 1050 Ixelles
Tue — Sat 11-21 Sun — Mon closed
200+ bottled beers, frites and cheese cutting boards.

Au Stomelings

Pl. de Londres 7, 1050 Ixelles
Mon — Sat 16.30-1 Sun closed
3 taps, 30+ bottled beers, snacks.

London Calling

Rue de Dublin 46, 1050 Ixelles
Mon — Fri 11.30-15/17-01 Sat 17-01 Sun closed
4 taps, 20+ bottled beers, snacks.

Other suggestions:

Ginette Bar

Pl. du Luxembourg 5, 1050 Ixelles
Mon — Sat 11-02
5 taps, 25+ bottled beers, restaurant.

Trendy resto-bar opened in 2018 that takes its name from the homonymous organic beer Ginette, around AB Inbev. They have a twin room on Rue du Bon Secours 4 in the city centre. Brussels.

The Pullman

Pl. du Luxembourg 12, 1050 Ixelles
Mon — Fri 9-23
10 taps, 25+ bottled beers, restaurant.

Interesting place due to the availability of American craft beers on tap and in bottles.

Public House 12

Pl. de Londres 12, 1050 Ixelles
Mon — Sun 10.30-12
10 taps, 25+ bottled beers, catering.

Classic pub to watch football or rugby matches with great burgers and good choice of beers.

BIA Mara

See restaurants page 279.

The Galia

Rue Jacques de Lalaing 22, 1040
Mon — Fri 8-22 Sat — Dom closed
6 taps, + 30 bottled beers, restaurant.

Brasserie nestled between the offices of the European Institutions and located behind the Hotel Thon a few steps from the Maelbeck metro stop. Outside the radar of visitors to Place Luxembourg, it also offers a good selection of Trappist beers.

The Horloge du Sud

See restaurants page 279.

Place Jourdan – Schuman

Welcome to the heart of the European Union! The Schuman rond-point is, geographically speaking, the crossroads of the palaces of the Institutions that populate the European Quarter. Divided by less than 100 metres from each other, there are the two main buildings of the European Commission (Berlaymont and Charlemagne), the buildings of the Council (Justus Lipsius, Lex and Europe) and that of the European External Action Service.

The best known, and which stands out most in the eyes, is undoubtedly the palace of Berlaymont. The palace is shaped like a cross, 55 meters high, divided into 18 floors (of which 4 are underground). Unlike all the other buildings of the institutions, it is not dedicated to one of the figures universally recognised as "fathers of Europe" but takes its name from the convent of nuns on whose site it is built. "Dames de Berlaymont" is in fact the name of the convent created in 1625 by the Countess de Berlaymont, Marguerite, and which until 1963 housed the college of women and located right where the main seat of the Commission now stands.

Your beer tour begins just below Berlaymont, more precisely at **Kitty O'Shea** where, according to many Irish living in Brussels, the best Guinness of Brussels is spilled. This area of the city is characterised by the presence of several Irish pubs. For inattentive eyes, they may all look the same, but that's not the case; each has its own characteristics, its rituals and its customers. They do not only pour Irish beers, but also several Belgian beers.

After savouring a pair of pints at Kitty O'Shea, take Rue Stevin and walk to the junction with Livingstone Avenue, turn left and across the street, at the corner of Rue Joseph II, you will find **The Wild Geese**. Among the Irish pubs of the city it is definitely the one I prefer for location, choice of beers and atmosphere. On site, order a Hopus, a generous blonde of the Lefebvre brewery.

From the Wild Geese, take the Chausse d'Etterbeek and walk for 5 minutes until you reach the Place Jean Rey. You will find yourself in front of a couple of futuristic glass buildings. One of them hosts your next stop: **Le Grand Central**.

It is a rather fashionable bar, on two floors, with two beautiful and large terraces overlooking the Parc Leopold and with interior design. Opened in 2017, it has taken inspiration from Brussels institution such as the Cafe Belga in Place Flagey, aiming to accommodate customers throughout the day, from breakfast to post-dinner drink. It is the right place to taste the Duvel 666, the new product of the giant Duvel-Moortgaat.

After leaving the Grand Central, cross the road and enter Parc Leopold.

This is the last oasis of peace in the frenetic European Quarter. In the second half of the nineteenth century, it housed a zoological garden. In 1880, it was acquired by the municipality of Brussels and opened to the public under the name Parc Leopold.

Today, it houses the Museum of the Institute of Natural Sciences, the famous Solvay Library, the high school, Emile Jacqmain, the House of the History of Europe, and the building of the Representation of the Lander of Bavaria to the European Institutions.

Walk along the pond inside the park (populated by numerous ducks) until the exit on Avenue du Maelbeek., from where you enter Place Jourdan.

The square owes its name to Dr. Jean-Baptiste Jourdan, patron of several hospices for the poor in the municipalities of Etterbeek and Ixelles.

The square has been recently renovated and almost totally pedestrianised. On Sunday, there is a very popular market. In the pre Covid era, every two years in October, the square hosted a local edition of the famous Oktoberfest.

What makes it famous in the world is the kiosk where many people consider the best "Frites" in Brussels (and therefore of the world) are to be found; Maison Antoine.

Founded in 1948 by Antoine Desmet, Maison Antoine has become known all over the world. During a break from one of the most difficult European Councils, that of Brexit in February 2016, former German Chancellor Angela Merkel was spotted lining up to buy a cone of the famous "Frites".

The square is surrounded by several bars and restaurants. Your first stop is **The First**, which together with another cafe just in front (L'Autobus), allows customers to sit at their tables (both indoors and outdoors) to consume their "Frites" after, of course, having ordered a drink. So, take your cone of fries sit in one of the tables of this timeless bar and order a wonderful Westmalle Triple.

Reinvigorated by your rich snack and famous Trappist beer, cross the road to the last stop of your tour; the **Beers Bank**, one of the most underrated bars in the city. A rich list (almost 200 beers), two floors (beautiful tavern) and a precise and punctual service. Close your beer tour with a Bush Ambree from the Dubuisson brewery!

Do not miss:

Kitty O'Shea

BD Charlemagne 42, 1040 Etterbeek
Mon — Sun 12-01
10 taps, 30+ bottled beers, snacks.

The Wild Geese

Avenue Livingstone 2/4, 1000 Brussels
Mon — Fri 16-01 Sat — Sun 12-01
14 taps, 30+ bottled beers, restaurant.

Grand Central

Rue Belliard 190, 1040 Etterbeek
Tue — Thu 12-00 Fri — Sat 12-1.30 Sun — Mon 12-23.30
8 taps, 8+ bottled beers, restaurant.

The First

PL. Jourdan 40, 1040 Etterbeek
Mon — Sun 8-23
7 taps, + 18 bottled beers, snacks.

Beer Banks

PL. Jourdan 34, 1040 Etterbeek
Mon — Fri 15-02 Sat — Sun 13-02
11 taps, + 150 bottled beers, snacks

Other suggestions:

L'Autobus

PL. Jourdan 33, 1040 Etterbeek
Mon — Sun 9-23
4 taps, 8+ bottled beers, snacks.

Together with The First, it allows customers to eat the "Frites" of the Maison Antoine upon order of drinks on site. Until the time pre Covid era, it was one of the best places in the area for prices and choice of beers. Now, position aside, the offer and the prices are no longer so agreeable.

Fat Boy's Sports Bar&Grill

Av. de Cortenbergh 36, 1000 Brussels
Closed Mon Sun — Thu 17-00 Fri 17-01 Sat 13-01 Sun 13-00
10 taps, 11+ bottled beers, restaurant.

Its 14 mega screens make it the most important sports pub in the city.

The Funky Monkey

Rue Archimède 65, 1000 Brussels
Mon 16-23 Mar — Sun 12-23
10 taps, 30+ bottled beers, restaurant.

Classic Irish pub with a large and beautiful back terrace.

The Hairy Canary

Rue Archimède 12, 1000 Brussels
Mon — Sun 12-23
8 taps, 10+ bottled beers, restaurant.

One of the oldest Irish/English pubs in the city.

James Joyce

Rue Archimède 34, 1000 Brussels
Mon — Fri 16-23 Sat — Sun 12-23
8 taps, 18+ bottled beers, restaurant.

Probably the most "Irish" Irish bar in Brussels.

The Terrasse

Av. des Celtes 1, 1040 Etterbeek
Mon — Sun 10-23
8 taps, 18+ bottled beers, restaurants.

Typical Belgian brasserie. The only place worth stopping for a drink in the elegant residential area of Merode, just outside the Cinquantenaire Park and a 10-minute walk from Schuman.

Schaerbeek

Schaerbeek is the second most populated municipality in the Brussels Capital Region, after Brussels-Ville, and the seventh most populated municipality in the whole of Belgium. It is located in the north-east of Brussels and incredibly is not yet connected to the rest of the city by any metro network (only by tram and bus).

It is a cosmopolitan municipality. This fact also influences its beer scene.

The suggested starting point for exploring Schaerbeek's beer scene is the **Python Bar**. Located on Avenue Emile Max, a stone's throw from Chasseurs Ardennais Square. On the square, every Friday there is one of the most interesting markets in the capital, with the possibility of drinking beers and craft ciders, and savouring tasty specialties from all over Europe at the various stalls.

The Python Bar opened in August 2018. The owner defined it as "neighbourhood bar" and offers an excellent choice of the better products in the world of craft beer, both on site and takeaway (there is a shop attached). Order a PAM, Pale Ale from the wide-ranging Atrium brewery.

Take Avenue Max until the intersection with Avenue Milcamps and turn right onto Rue Victor Hugo. Walk for 5 minutes through Chausse de Louvain, another of the city's most important and busy roads. After crossing it, Rue Victor Hugo becomes Grand Rue au Bois, turn to the first street on the left, Rue Jacques Jansen, where at number 3 you will find the first and only Cider bar in Brussels: **Joran**.

This book is dedicated to beer, but many beer lovers are also fond of cider (like myself). Cider developed as a niche drink but is now increasingly present at different latitudes.

Joran is the right place to explore this very interesting world as well as a pleasant stopover between one beer and another. Joran, the owner, made the brave choice to jump in the world of cider in the middle of the capital of beers...what a great story! Ask for advice from the owner and order a Belgian cider, there are many good ones.

From Joran, take Avenue Chazaland walk for 10 minutes and then turn left into Rue Paul Devigne and then immediately right onto Rue Henri Stacquet. At the corner with the Avenue Jan Stobbaerts, you will find your next stop: the **1030 Cafe**.

The name 1030 refers to Schaerbeek's postal code. The café was opened in October 2016 by two brothers, Guillaume and Max, and quickly became a meeting place for this area that lacks venues with good craft beers.

They work a lot with local breweries such as Brasserie de la Mule or Brasserie La Source. Order a Python, a double IPA by Brasserie de La Source.

From 1030, walk through the Square Prevost-Delaunay. You will find yourself in front of the Parc Josaphat which, with its 20 hectares, is the green lung of Schaerbeek as well as one of the most interesting parks in Brussels.

The park was created in 1904 on the initiative of a landscape designer, Edmond Galoppin, and throughout the time it has undergone various transformations.

Walk along the park, first along Avenue General Eisenhower, then Avenue des Azalees, then Avenue Paul Deschanel and finally Avenue Louis Bertrand. In a 15-minute walk, you will reach **Le Barboteur**, located at number 23 of the latter street.

Opened in May 2015, the Barboteur calls itself a "Birroteque". In fact, in addition to being a well-stocked beer shop of Belgian and European craft beers it is also a meeting place for beer enthusiasts and a neighbourhood bar. Together with the Dynamo Bar, it is the real novelty of the Brussels beer scene becoming the frontrunner of a new concept; the spread of non-Belgian craft beers in the capital.

Sebastien, the owner, together with Greg of the Dynamo Bar is one of the creators and organisers of the SWAFF Beer Festival.

At the Barboteur, opt for one of the foreign beers on tap, or for a Pumba Stout, the new stout of Brasserie Minne.

The Barboteur is located in the heart of what has become the Turkish soul of Brussels. Around 142,000 Turks live in the Brussels Region and Schaerbeek is home to a vibrant community. There are plenty of Turkish restaurants and grocery shops and the Turkish flag hangs from many windows and balconies.

From Avenue Louis Bertrand, turn right into Chausse de Haecht and follow it to the intersection. Then take the first street on the right, Rue Rubens and reach number 95 where you will find your last stop; the **Brasserie de la**

Mule. Here, you will be easily come across live music, in an atmosphere totally different from the one you find in the surrounding streets. At Brasserie de la Mule, you are in Belgium, but you drink German style beers. So, forget the full-body Belgian beers and get thrown into very interesting interpretations of Lager, Kolsh and Altbier of Brasserie de la Mule.

Do not miss:

Python Beer Cellar

AV. Emile Max 55, 1030 Schaerbeek
Mon — Sat 16-01 Sun closed
8 taps, 80+ bottled beers, snacks.

Joran Cidrothèque

Rue Jacques Jansen 3, 1030 Schaerbeek
Mon — Sun closed Wed — Thu 16-00 Fri — Sat 16-01
Sun 16-23

1030 Café

AV. Jan Stobbaerts 100, 1030 Schaerbeek
Sun — Mon 16-23 Mar — Thu 16-01 Fri — Sat 16-03
3 taps, 20+ bottled beers, snacks.

Le Barboteur Bierotheque

AV. Louis Bertrand 23, 1030 Schaerbeek
Tue — Thu 15-0.30 Fri — Sat 15-1.30 Sun 15-00 Mon closed
20 taps, 150+ bottled beers, snacks.

Brasserie de la Mule

See breweries page 82.

Other suggestions:

Copain

AV. Rogier 262, 1030 Schaerbeek
Mon — Thu 16-01 Fri 16-03 Sat 18-03 Dom closed
5 taps, 20+ bottled beers, snacks.

The Copain is a nice neighbourhood wine bar, located not far from the 1030 Café with an interesting selection of craft beers. They offer delicious cold cuts and cheese.

Café Coteaux

Rue des Coteaux 160, 1030 Schaerbeek
Mon — Sun 7.30-01
3 taps, 10+ bottles, snacks.
In the beer desert of the area around Place Dailli, it is probably the best choice. Next to the classic industrial beers, a good choice of Trappist beers such as Orval and Rochefort.

Le Wappers

Place Wappers 7, 1030 Schaerbeek
Tue - Thu 16 – 00 Fri – Sat 16 – 01 Sun – Mon closed
4 taps, + 20 bottled beers, restaurant.

Le Wappers is being brought back to life by Bernard Leboucq, one of the owners of Brasserie de la Senne who is particularly active within his neighbourhood.
The laminated drinks menu with a neo-propagandist design by the excellent graphic artist Jean Goovaerts,

informed us that Gustave Wappers (1803-1874) was the official painter of king Leopold I, which is appropriate because this establishment is as picturesque as can be.

Beers from Brasserie de la Senne, Trappist and "classics" such as Rodenbach. The place also offers a range of unpretentious snacks.

L'âne verte

See restaurants page 279.

Gare Centrale – Congrès

During your stay in Brussels, you will surely pass through the Central Station (Gare Centrale). Although it has only six tracks, it is the second busiest station in the country after the Gare du Midi. Often, during peak hours on working days, trains follow each other minute after minute. It is the main hub for the north-south link of Belgium.

The building was designed by famous architect Victor Horta in the 1930s and completed by Maxime Brunfaut in 1952. The main facade is adorned with 9 large windows that symbolise the then nine provinces of Belgium.

A curiosity related to the Central Gare is that the station has, on the Cantersteen side, access to a waiting room used by Royals (not so often, the last time seems to be in 1958 for a visit of the Queen to the Netherlands).

Right in front of the Gare Centrale, you will find the Brussels **Brewdog**.

In 2015, the famous Scottish brewery arrived in Brussels, the capital of beer. It is the first bar dedicated to foreign beers to open in the city after the Danish Tavern (now closed), a tough choice that seems to be paying.

The place is very large and modern, with a minimalist decor and a beautiful terrace overlooking the spire of the Grand Place. 40 taps, some dedicated to small Belgian craft breweries.

My only complaint: prices are really high for these latitudes. It will be a long and challenging ride so limit yourself to a pint of Vagabond Pale Ale.

From Brewdog, go up the Boulevard de l'Empress, leaving Gare Central behind on the right and then continue uphill along Rue des Colonies. At the junction with Rue Royale, go left and turn to the second street on the right, Rue de l'Enseignment. At number 57, you will find one of the beer institutions of the city; the **Bier Circus**.

Opened in 1993 by Patrick D'hane, one of the gurus of Belgian beer, it is one of the best places to taste a good beer, or to try some beer recipes (it is also a brasserie). Some years ago, it also opened a beer shop in the countryside, in the locality of Saint-Sauveur, on the French-Flemish language frontier of Belgium, with more than 250 beers. Order a Hommelbier from Brasserie Leroy from Watou and match it with its delicious paté.

Leave the Bier Circus, continue on Rue de l'Enseignment, cross rue du Congres and stop at the Place de la Libertè.

The square is located in the centre of an urbanisation plan, developed by architect Antoine Mennessier in 1875, crossed by a main axis leading to the Column of Congress and two diagonal axes (rue de l'Enseignement — rue des Cultes, rue de la Presse, rue de l'Association) that indicate the four fundamental freedoms set out in the Belgian Constitution at the time of independence.

The buildings that surround the square are the work of the architect, Wynand Janssens, who made it uniform and symmetrical in the eclectic style inspired by the Renaissance. Under the ox eye of the 7 pediments crowning the stills there is a five-pointed star symbolising perfection. Also at ornamental level, the angels seen on the pediments are all similar, while the figures around the windows are all different.

In the middle of the square, surrounded by trees, stands the statue of Charles Rogier, one of the leaders of the Revolution of 1830 that led the country to independence.

In Place de la Liberteè, you will find the **Cafe Caberdouche**.

The name "Caberdouche" was used to refer to bars of dubious reputation in Brussels popular neighbourhoods that housed women of pleasure. Over time, its meaning evolved to become synonymous with cabaret or cafe.

It is a very nice place, with a good selection of beers and wines and with homemade dishes. The right place to enjoy an IPA Lantern of Brasserie L'Ermitage.

Your tour is not over yet. Go back to your steps to Rue de l'Enseignment, pass in front of the Bier Circus (trying not to go back inside) and reach, at number 27, the Restaurant **La Tana**.

La Tana is a small Roman restaurant. The atmosphere is cosy and familiar, and the food is very good. But La Tana is also one of the best places in Brussels to try special beers from Italy and all over Europe. Valerio, the owner, is a great beer connoisseur and a visit to his restaurant, as well as leaving your belly full, will also be very interesting from the beer point of view due to the excellent choice on site. With Valerio, it will be difficult for you to limit yourself to only one beer... in any case order one of the very interesting products of the German brewery Kemker Kultuur. The rest will come by itself!

Do not miss:

BrewDog Brussels

Putterie 20, 1000 Brussels
Mon — Sun 12-23.30
40 taps, 50+ bottled beers, restaurant.

Bier Circus

Rue de l'Enseignement 57, 1000 Brussels
Tue — Fri 15-23 Sat — Mon closed
5 taps, 250+ bottled beers, restaurant.

Cafe Caberdouche

Pl. de la Liberté 8, 1000 Brussels
Mon — Sun 11.30-01
10 taps, 20+ bottled beers, snacks.

La Tana

Rue de l'Enseignement 27, 1000 Brussels
Tue — Sat 12-21 Sun — Mon closed
4 taps, 60+ bottled beers, restaurant.

Other suggestions:

Laurent Gerbaud Chocolatier

Rue Ravenstein 2D, 1000 Brussels

Tue — Sun 12-18 Mon closed

A chocolate shop in a beer guide? Yes, yes! It is, in my humble opinion, the best artisan chocolate shop in Brussels. Laurent Gerbaud, the Maître chocolatier, is a great expert and passionate about beers. In its menu you can find several products of Brasserie de la Senne. It also organises a workshop to match chocolate-beer.

Historic centre

The historic centre of Brussels is also its beating heart. Geographically speaking, the "centre" of Brussels is bordered by a ring road of large avenues called "Petit Ring". The locals define the area as "Pentagone".

The centre of Brussels is also the part of the city called "lower city", divided by the "high city" by the Mont des Arts, the small urban hill that descends from Place Royal towards Boulevard de L'Impereur.

This area has the highest concentration of bars and restaurants in the city. For this reason, I have divided it into three possible itineraries: Grand Place, Saint Catherine — Saint Gery — Boulevard Anspach and Place Jeu de Balles-Marolle.

It is the most touristic area of the city. Especially during the weekend, these are very crowded venues. Keep this in mind when planning your travel.

Grand Place

Your tour starts from one of the historic venues of the Belgian capital: **À la Mort Subite**. The origin of this curious name is to be found in 1910 when Theophile Vossen was the owner of a place called "La Cour Royale". Among his clients, there was a group of employees of the National Bank of Belgium who spent their time in the premises playing a card game called "421". Each time, before returning to the office, they played one last quick game. The player who lost was called "the sudden death".

When Mr. Vossen moved the restaurant to the current site, he decided to call the local "À la Mort Subite" which was the same name as the beers he produced.

The decor, in Louis XIII style, has never changed giving it an atmosphere of old times that makes it very popular among tourists.

To honour this historic place and the city of Brussels, order a Faro on tap, accompanied by one of the house's excellent omelettes.

Leaving À la Mort Subite, take the beautiful Galeries Royales Saint-Hubert. They have two hundred metres of windows and they are divided into 3 sections; the Galerie de la Reine, the Galerie du Roi and the Galerie des Princes. Once named the "Parapluie de Bruxelles" — (the Brussels umbrella), the Galleries were designed by the architect Cluysenaer in 1837.

As you walk through the Galeries, you will pass in front of the various boutiques; famous brands, fashion designers, antique or modern art shops, a glove shop, a hat and umbrella shop, a jewellery, a bookshop, various chocolate shops, restaurants, a cinema and a theatre.

The Grand Place (Grote Markt in Dutch) is the geographical, historical and commercial heart of Brussels, as well as being one of the most famous squares in Europe. The square is part of a 17th century architectural complex.

Exit from the Galleries, turn right into Rue du Marchè Aux Herbes and then immediately left, through a narrow street called Rue des Harengs. Immediately on the left, you will find your second stop; **Family Brews**.

Located a few steps from the Grand Place, in a 17th century UNESCO-protected building, it has been recently renovated. On the ground floor, there is the real bar while upstairs a meeting room for events or tastings. The choice is really good and the three passionate owners are always ready to suggest tasty combinations with the delicious cheeses of "La Frutierie". On site, order a Kana blonde from the Flemish brewery Kana.

Leaving the Family Brew, in a few steps you will reach the magnificent Grand Place, which I personally consider the most beautiful square in Europe.

The Grand Place is part of an impressive architectural complex, fascinating for any visitor. Struck by such beauty, it is difficult to decide where to direct your gaze. Even today, after more than 10 years, every time I pass I stop to admire it and to take a picture.

In 1695, the cannons of the French army destroyed most of the buildings in the square. Most were later completely rebuilt, except for the Town Hall.

The Grand Place is surrounded by the houses of the guilds, the Hôtel de Ville and the Maison du Roi. Among the most significant buildings we find;

Hotel de Ville; Located southeast of the square, the Town Hall is the most important and ancient architectural jewel of the Grand Place. Its tower of 96 meters, dated 1459, is surmounted by a statue of Saint Michael. The roof of the Hotel de Ville is perforated by dozens of skylights.

Maison du Roi; The House of the King was built in 1536 and was destroyed in 1873. For many years, it was the residence of the monarchs, while today it houses the Museum of the City (Musée de la Ville), where artifacts from the 16th century are displayed, such as paintings, carpets and clothes of the Manneken Pis.

Maison des Ducs de Brabant; Between numbers 14 and 19 of the square, there is this neoclassical architectural complex with Flemish stylistic roots, composed by the six houses of the guild.

Le Pigeon; Between numbers 26 and 27 of the square there is Le Pigeon, the house where Victor Hugo lived in 1852 during his exile in Belgium.

For us, the beer lovers, at number 10 there is L'Arbre d'or (the Golden Tree), House of the Brewers Corporation. Today, it hosts the Beer Museum with a reconstruction of an 18th century brewery and ancient tools. The building dated 1696 and is adorned with sculptures by Marc de Vos and Pierre van Dievoet. The House is topped by the equestrian statue of Charles Alexander of Lorraine, in place of that of Maximilian II Emanuele of Bavaria, governor of the Spanish Netherlands at the time of the reconstruction of Brussels.

Drinking on the Grand Place may be expensive, but also has its charm. At number 1, you will find the House of the Bakers Corporation. It was built in 1696-97 by Jean Cosyn. It features a classic three-order façade crowned with statues and octagonal dome with copper cladding. At the centre of the façade, there is the sculptural group with the bust of Charles II of Spain that gives its name to the building. Originally, the three bays to the right constituted a detached house, the Saint-Jacques (San Giacomo), with access from Rue au Beurre. The building, much altered over the centuries, was entirely rebuilt between 1901 and 1902 on the original seventeenth-century projects.

In this building, there is **Le Roy d'Espagne**, the most famous bar on the Grand Place, which offers a wonderful panoramic view of the square. Enjoy the atmosphere with a Rochefort 8.

From the Grand Place, proceed towards Rue de la Tete d'or passing by the famous Hotel Amigo, at the junction with Rue du Lombard turn left. You will find yourself facing the **Nüetnigenough**, and since you may be hungry keep in mind that it is one of the best beer restaurants in the city. Continuing on Rue de Lombard turn to the first street on the right, Rue de l'Etuve.

On your left, surrounded by group of tourists with cameras, there is the famous Manneken Pis.

It is a small statue of about fifty centimetres that depicts a naked boy, urinating from the top of a fountain. Since the 14th century, it is one of the most representative and beloved symbols of Brussels.

The Manneken Pis was carved in stone in 1388. He suffered several theft attempts. After a successful one, it was decided to place, on the fountain, a bronze copy of the original stone statue, made in 1619 by Jérôme Duquesnoy, a famous Belgian artist of the time. This statue also suffered various attempts at theft. Today it is not actually known whether it is the copy made by Duquesnoy or a further copy.

There are various legends about the origin of the statue; for some it represents a boy who extinguished a flame by urinating on it, thus saving the city from a fire. For others, the boy represents the son of Godofredo III of Lorraine who, before the battle of Ransbeke in1142 hung the baby's cradle to a tree. The baby got out during the battle and urinated on the tree. Or again, he represents the son of a nobleman from Brussels who, abandoning a procession to urinate on the wall of a witch's house, was transformed into a statue by the same witch by a curse.

You will have time to reflect about your favourite option in front of a Pater Lieven Triple at **Poechenellekelder**.

"Poechenelle" in local dialect means small puppet. It is a place of old times, one of the best preserved examples of what was an Estaminet Bruxellois. The place is very beautiful and appreciated by both locals and tourists. It is decorated with puppets of all kinds.

From Poechenellekelder, proceed on Rue du Chene to Place de la Vieille Halle aux Bles. In the middle of the square you will find the statue of Jacques Brel, the famous Belgian singer-songwriter, poet and actor. Right in front of the statue there is your next stop; the **Gist**.

The Gist was opened in December 2017 by Jenlain Delcourt, former bartender of the Moeder Lambic and his partner Jody Lecieux. It seemed to have almost closed down due to the economic crisis caused by the Covid pandemic but, in the end, it has managed to survive.

It is an ideal place for music lovers (there is an impressive choice of vinyls) but especially for lovers of Cask Ale. In fact, the counter has 4 pumps where local or export casks are finely poured. Order a Heavy Porter from the Brussels brewery No Science, the cask version is phenomenal.

You've seen many places but your tour is not still over. I deliberately left to the end the most famous place when we talk about in the centre of Brussels: the **Delirium Cafe**.

The Delirium is the classic place- either you love it or hate it. Personally, leaving apart the chaos that distinguishes it (in the evening during the weekend it is terrible), I consider it a must for any lover of good Belgian beers.

The advice is to go there in the afternoon to be able to appreciate the wide choice.

From the Gist walk straight (if you are still able), cross Rue del'Hopital and Place Saint.Jeanne, turn on Rue de la Violette and then right on Rue des Chapeliers, arrive at the Grand Place (which you will never tire admiring), after the Hotel de Ville turns on Petite Rue des Bouchers (which then becomes Impasse Schuddeveld) and you will find yourself in Rue des Bouchers. It is the fish restaurant street, a true tourist trap. Turn down on Impasse de la Fidelitè and welcome to the Delirum Village!

Here, you have plenty of choice between **Delirium Cafe, Monasterium, Hoppy Loft, Taphouse or Floris Bar**.

Head to the bottom left, in front of the little sister of Manneken, the Janneken Pis, where the Delirium café is located. On the ground floor, order a Delirium Tremens followed by a Guillottine. Then, go down the stairs, ask "Le Livre s'il vous plait" (the menu, a real book, where the 2000 beers available on site are listed) and choose the next one. You are in Brussels, you are at the Delirium, you are at the centre of the Beer Capital.

Do not miss:

À la Mort Subite

Rue Montagne aux Herbes Potagères 7, 1000 Brussels
Mon — Sat 11.30-00 Sun closed
8 taps, 25+ bottled beers, restaurant.

Family Brews

Rue des Harengs 2, 1000 Brussels
Mon — Wed 16–02 Thu 14-02 Fri 14-04 Sat 11-04 Sun 11-02
60+ bottled beers, snacks.

The Roy d'Espagne

Grand Place 1, 1000 Brussels
Mon — Sun 10-00
11 taps, 25+ bottled beers, restaurant.

Poechenellekelder

Rue du Chêne 5, 1000 Brussels
Tue — Sun 11-01 Fri — Sat 11-02 Mon Closed
5 taps, 80+ bottled beers, snacks.

Gist

Pl. de la Vieille Halle aux Blés 30, 1000 Brussels
Sun — Closed Mon Mar — Sat 16-00
16 taps, 4 pumps, 40+ bottled beers, snacks.

Delirium Village

Imp. de la Fidélité 4, 1000 Brussels
Mon — Thu 12-03 Fri — Sat 12-04 Sun 12-02

Composed of: Delirium Cafe Brussels, Delirium
Taphouse, Delirium Hoppy Loft, Delirium Monasterium,
Floris Bar, Floris Garden, Floris Tequila

Other suggestions:

À la Bécasse

Rue de Tabora 11, 1000 Brussels
Tue — Sun 11-23 Mon closed
10 taps, 30+ bottles, restaurant.

One of the first Estaminet of the city having been opened
in 1877. It specialises in serving Lambic, Geuze and
Kriek of Timmermans in traditional lambic jars.

A' l'image Notre Dame

Rue du Marchè Aux Herbes 8, 1000 Brussels
Mon — Wed 11-01 Thu — Sat 11-03 Sun 11-01
4 taps, 30+ bottles, snacks.

One of the historic "estaminet" of the city centre founded in 1884. To reach it you need to go deeper into the characteristic Impasse des Cadeaux. Warm and friendly atmosphere. Among the many interesting beers, try the "Mijole", the shot of the house.

Au Bon Vieux Temps

Impasse Saint Nicolas 8/4, 1000 Brussels
Sun — Fri 11-23 Sat 15-23
4 taps, 15+ bottles, snacks.

Another historic Brussels estaminet located in an "Impasse" (road without exit) a stone's throw from the Grand Place. Inside it seems to be in a Gothic church. If you order a "Chevalier" you will be served a one-litre beer in a glass 50 centimetres high.

Little Delirium Café

Rue du Marché aux Fromages 9, 1000 Brussels
30 taps, 200+ bottles

A concentrate of everything you find, and drink, at Delirium Village.

Au Brasseur

Rue du Marché aux Fromages 3, 1000 Brussels
Mon — Sun 09-23
15 taps, 50+ bottled beers, snacks

Very touristic place but with a very good choice of beers.

Beer Capital

Boulevard Anspach 89, 1000 Brussels.

Mon — Sun 10-05
16 taps, 700 + bottles, snacks.

Very recent addition to the already rich panorama of the city centre. Very rich choice of beers.

Nüetnigenough

See restaurants page 279.

Manneken Pis Café

Rue des Grands Carmes 31/33, 1000 Brussels
Mon — Thu 13-00 Fri — Sun 12-00
14 taps, 11+ bottles, snacks

Located in front of the famous statuette of Manneken Pis. Duvel-Moortgaat single-brand bar with all the beers in the range. For lovers of Duvel, it is the only place in Brussels where you can find it on tap.

The Cercle des Voyageurs

Rue des Grands Carmes 19, 1000 Brussels
Mon — Sun 11-00
3 taps, 10+ bottles, restaurant.

It is a real "Art and Travel Café" that hosts exhibitions and conferences. The environment is very charming, decorated with old suitcases and vintage maps.

Estaminet du The", "Tre Royal de Toone"

Rue du Marché Aux Herbes 66, 1000 Brussels
5 taps, 40+ bottled beers

The Royal Theatre Toone is a folk puppet theatre. Opened in 1830 it is the only puppet theatre still active. It was originally located in the Marolles district and only in 1966 moved near the Grand Place. The shows are mainly held in the Brussels dialect. The theatre is equipped with a beautiful estaminet with an excellent choice of beers.

Wolf

Rue du Fossé aux Loups 50, 1000 Brussels
Mon — Sun 12-23
Covered market with several street food stands. Here, you can find "Flow", a beer brewed on site, beers from Brasserie Belgoo, located just outside Brussels.

Café Métropole

Place de Brouckère 31, Brussels, Belgium

The café-bar of the Hôtel Métropole with its beautifully decorated ceilings, huge crystal chandeliers, giant windows, chairs covered with red leather and elegant coordinated lamps, is a historic place that has recently reopened. We do not go for the menu but for the historic atmosphere of a Brussels that is no longer there.

Boulevard Anspach — Saint Gery — Saint Catherine

Boulevard Anspach is an important boulevard in the centre of Brussels, connecting Place de Brouckère to Place Fontainas. It is dedicated to Jules Anspach, former mayor of Brussels. The River Senne once flowed here, but is now covered over.

Until 2015, the avenue was one of the busiest arteries of Brussels. After a long debate, it was pedestrianised, restoring some tranquillity to a district already stressed by wild nightlife, thus providing Brussels citizens with a large pedestrian area like a real European capital.

Your tour will start from Place Fontainas and the renowned **Moeder Lambic Fontainas**.

The Moeder Lambic Fontainas is the second location of Chez Moeder Lambic. It was inaugurated in 2006 after the great success of the Moeder Lambic in St. Gilles. The aim was to serve more tourists due to its location just a few steps from the Bourse and the Grand Place.

Both locations are renowned for their excellent selection of Lambic and Gueuze and host the Cantillon Zwanze Day, every year at the end of September. Moeder Lambic has also an excellent selection of Belgian and foreign beers. To start your tour in the best manner, order an evergreen Kriek from Cantillon, served here with a pump tap system.

From the Moeder Lambic, walk along Boulevard Anspach to the Bourse. The Belgian Beer World will be opened in 2023 in the Bourse building. It will be a visitor centre entirely dedicated to Belgian beers.

The renovations started in 2020, but since the building is a UNESCO monument, they are taking longer than usual. The beer museum is set to become a major tourist attraction with 400,000 expected visitors per year. This is a project very much sought by the Belgian beer sector. Over a hundred Belgian breweries have invested a total of more than 5 million euros in the project.

From Place de La Bourse, take Rue Jules Van Praet, a street characterised by the presence of many Asian restaurants, and go to Place Saint-Géry.

Place Saint-Géry is the heart of the first inhabited settlement of Brussels. In 979, Duke Charles of Lower Lotaringia built a castle on the Isle of the Senne and a chapel dedicated to Saint Gery where the relics of Gudule of Brussels were kept. This island was located where the square is today.

In the sixteenth century, the chapel was replaced by a church in late Gothic style with the same name. The church was then demolished during the French occupation in 1797. In its place, a fountain was built that today is located in the centre of the Halles Saint-Géry. Les Halles are a Neo-Renaissance building built by architect Adolphe

Vanderheggen. After that the river Senne[13] was covered over in 1881. Until 1977, it was a vegetable market. Today it houses an exhibition space and a bar, the **Café des Halles**, which is your next stop.

At Caffè des Halles, you can have a beer relaxing on a leather armchair, or on a deckchair, while listening to live music. On a weekend evening, get ready for a long queue because the place is always crowded. Order a Triple Saint-Gery, the beer made by Bobby brewery in honour of the district.

Today the district of Saint-Gery is at the heart of the Brussels nightlife with clubs open until late at night and many, perhaps too many, people.

From Place Saint-Gery, take Rue du Pont de la Carpe and then turn left onto Rue Auguste Orts heading towards the Bourse. On the right, at number 14, you will find your next stop: **Le Coq**.

Le Coq is a typical Brussels bistro much valued by the Belgians inhabitants of the capital. The interior is characterised by the classic wooden interior and the atmosphere is always cheerful thanks to the varied customers who frequent it. Sometimes, you can also find live music and the choice of beer is very good. Order a Troubadour Magma brewed by The Musketeers brewery.

From Le Coq, retrace your steps on rue Auguste Orts and turn to the first right on Rue des Poissoniers and then immediately left on Rue Sainte-Catherine continuing to number 42 where you will find the **Monk**.

---

[13]   From 9AM to 4Pm, at number 23 of the Place you can enter into a small courtyard where it was rebuilt an old dock of the Senne River.

It is a place not to be missed in Brussels. However, finding a table might be very difficult because so often it is full of people.

Colourful tiled floors, wooden benches and walls covered with mirrors, furthermore, and if you are lucky, there might be improvised performances on the piano, all making the Monk a unique place of its kind.

The choice of beer reflects expectations and if you are hungry, you can order a "pistolet" (sausage sandwich), or a slice of a tasty Belgian cheese. Order a Monk's Stout from Dupont.

Leaving Monk, turn the corner, you will find yourself in Place Sainte-Catherine, one of the most iconic places in the city.

The most interesting cultural reference is the church of Sainte-Catherine. Built in the 15th century, the church is a mixture of different styles. Its Victorian interior captures attention and the Gothic-style facade is crowned with mischievous gargoyles. During the festivities, when the characteristic "Christmas Markets" are organised in Brussels, a show of lights is projected on the walls of the church. The admission to the church is for free and usually it hosts interesting collections of paintings.

The main part of the square, where the Anspach Fountain is located, has always been one of the favourite places for young people to meet. When the weather is good (but also when it is not so good...we are in Belgium where the sun is not considered necessary to go out and socialise) many people sit on the edges of the fountains for hours chatting and drinking a beer, among the aromas of the many fish restaurants for which the square is famous.

The square was once covered with water, being one of the three basins of the canal connecting Brussels to Willebroek. And your last stop on this tour is dedicated to the ancient basin: **Au Bassin**.

Located at number 74 of Quai aux Briques, it occupies the premises of an old industrial building. Until February 2020, it was known as Via Café.

It is a very busy but also very extensive place, with several very spacious rooms, so it is quite easy to find a place even during weekend evenings. The beer menu is remarkable, with a strong focus on Brussels breweries. Order an "Au Bassin", the house beer produced by The Musketeers.

Do not miss:

Moeder Lambic Fontainas

PL. Fontainas 8, 1000 Brussels
Mon — Thu 16-00 Fri 16-01 Sat 14-01 Sun 14-23
20 taps, 100+ bottled beers, snacks.

Café des Halles

PL. Saint-Géry 1, 1000 Brussels
Mon — Sun 11-22
7 taps, 20+ bottled beers, snacks.

Le Coq

Rue Auguste Orts 14, 1000 Brussels
Mon — Sat 12-01 Sun 15-01
3 taps, 40+ bottled beers, snacks

Billie (ex Monk)

Rue Sainte-Catherine 42, 1000 Bruxelles
Mon – Wed 11-00 Thu 11-01 Fri – Sat 11-02 Sun 13-00
11 taps, +60 bottles, food

Au Bassin

Quai aux Briques 74, 1000 Brussels
Tue -Wed 16-01 Thu -Sat 16.30-2.30 Sun-Mon 16-01
12 taps, 25+ bottled beers, snacks.

Other suggestions:

Bar du Canal

Rue Antoine Dansaert 208, 1000 Brussels
Mon closed Mar — Sun 17-23
1 tap, 10+ bottled beers, snacks.

Wine bar with canal view and with a limited, but very
interesting, list of beers.

Café Walvis

Rue Antoine Dansaert 209, 1000 Brussels
6 taps, 20+ bottled beers, restaurant.

Very nice Café/Brasserie right in front of the Brussels
Beer Project. Good choice of beers from Brussels.

Brussels Beer Project Dansaert

Rue Antoine Dansaert 188, 1000 Brussels
Closed Mon Tue — Fri 17-23 Sat 14-23.30

Historical tap room of the Brussels Beer Project, today dedicated to the Lambic project.

Barbeton

Rue Antoine Dansaert 114, 1000 Brussels
Mon — Tue 8-23 Wed — Fri 08-01 Sat 10-01 Sun 10-23
5 taps, 15+ bottled beers, snacks.

Classic corner bar and gem of the Dansaert area. Cosy environment and good choice of beers.

Brasserie Surrealiste

See page 90.

Daringman

Rue de Flandre 37, 1000 Brussels
Mon — Sat 13-03 Sun closed
4 taps, 10 + bottled beers, snacks.

One of the last "Bruin cafes" in the area of Saint-Catherine. Average menu but very characteristic atmosphere. The polyglottal Martine, owner of the restaurant, welcomes every customer with kindness and sympathy.

Bar des Amis

Rue Sainte-Catherine 30, 1000 Brussels
Mon — Wed 17-02 Thu 17-03 Fri — Sat 16-04 Sun 16-01
5 taps, 30+ bottled beers, snacks.

The chain is present in several cities in Belgium. It's a good alternative if you don't find a place at Monk.

Greenwich Café

Rue des Chartreux 7, 1000 Brussels
Mon — Closed Sea Wed — Sun 11.45-00
5 taps, 15+ bottled beers, restaurant.

It is a historic place whose fame is due to the fact that Magritte came there to play chess with other important figures from the Surrealist scene in Brussels. It's worth having a drink therer just for its interior.

Les Brasseurs

BD Anspach 77, 1000 Brussels
Mon — Thu 10-1.30 Fri — Sat 10-2.30 Sun 11-1.30
6 taps, 30+ bottled beers, snacks.
Good option during the day thanks to the good choice of beers. In the evening, it becomes a dance floor with DJ.

Bélier Bar

Borgwal 9, 1000 Brussels
Tue — Thu 17-02 Fri — Sat 17-04
6 taps, 30+ bottled beers, snacks.

Cocktail bar with a very interesting menu of beers. On tap, it is easy to find beer brewed in collaboration with Brasserie La Source.

Cafe Lutgarde - Dansaert

Rue du Rem des Moines 3, 1000 Bruxelles
Tue 15-00 Wed – Sat 15-01 Sun 14-23 Mon closed
7 taps, x bottles, food.

Opened in 2020, it is one of the two city taprooms of the young Abbaye d'Aywiers brewery (located in the town of

Lasne). Five of the seven taps are dedicated to their 'Lutgarde' brand of beers (which, despite their name, are not typical 'abbey' styles), the other two rotate with microbreweries from Brussels. Large selection of bottled beers.

Au Laboreur

Rue de Flandre 108, 1000 Bruxelles
Mon – Sun 10-00
5 taps, +20 bottles, snacks.
The building housing Au Laboureur café is a modest Art Deco style corner property, featuring five levels, a side hall and two wings under a gabled roof. The ground floor of the property, which is allocated for hospitality, includes an entrance in the central hall.

Constructed in 1927, the building became a key part of the café scene from its inception, originally under the name of Brasserie Carlier. Two years later, in 1929, the café adopted its current name, Brasserie Au Laboureur.

The Brussels-Capital Region Government has classed the Au Laboureur café as a protected monument of the city.

It has preserved the relaxed charm of old Brussels even if the neighbourhood has become quite hipster. The interior is decorated with antique beer signs, round mirrors and an old telephone booth.

Café Lava

Rue Saint-Christophe 20, 1000 Brussels
Mon — Thu 15-01 Fri 15-03 Sat — Sun 16-01
5 taps, 30+ bottled beers, snacks.

Classic corner bar revisited in modern style. Good choice of beers and evenings with live music.

Nightshop

Rue de flandres 167, 1000 Bruxelles
Thu 17-23 Fri – Sat 12 – 23

Nightshop is a big warehouse with as many boxes of wines as they are people. Industrial shelves at the back, a giant bar slash open kitchen and an excellent selection of "whales" not easy to find even in you live in Belgium (Bofkont, Bokke, h.ertie, Pellicle, Antidoot) unfortunately to drink only on site.

In't Spinnekopke

See restaurants page 279.

Boulangerie Pinpin

Rue Blaes 152, 1000 Bruxelles
Thu – Sat 08-18 Sun 08-13 Mon – Wed closed

Located in the district of Marolles, it is a bakery/cellar, a unique concept of its kind. Alongside the traditional products of a bakery, you can buy craft beers and wines. Here you can find the spontaneous fermentation products of Osma BXL.

La Fruitière

Rue du Marché au Charbon Kolenmarkt 99/103
Sun — Mon closed Tue — Sat 11-19

First "Bar à fromage" of the Belgian capital. It was opened by a French couple from the Jura region. It offers a very rich variety of cheese, mostly Belgian and French. They usually have Cantillon's Gueuze and Brasserie de l'Ermitage beers on tap.

Café Bizon

Rue du Pont de la Carpe 7, 1000 Brussels
Mon — Thu 16-02 Fri — Sat 16-04 Dom closed
4 taps, 20+ bottles, snacks.

Cowboy\Westerns themed two-floors venue with live music. Good choice of beers and cocktails.

Booze'n Blues

Rue des Riches Claires 20, 1000 Brussels
Tue — Sat 17-23.30 Sun — Mon closed
4 taps, 20+ bottles.

Little jewel hidden behind St. Gery. The owner, Eddy, has equipped it with a beautiful Jukebox and has an impressive collection of vinyls. On the ceiling, you can see an original piece of the Atomium, built in aluminium in 1958 and then renovated in steel. Excellent selection of beers and Genevier.

Au Soleil

Rue du Marché au Charbon Kolenmarkt 86, 1000 Brussels
Mon — Thu 9.30-01 Fri — Sat 9.30-02 Sun 9.30-00
7 taps, 10+ bottles.

Classic Brussels café with wooden interiors and a beautiful terrace on the pedestrian street in front of the church of Notre Dame des Bons Secours.

Place Jeu de Balles — Marolles — Sablon

Jeu de Balles Square is one of the most iconic places in Brussels. It is located in the popular district of Marolles. On the evening of July 20, the eve of the National Festival of 21 July, the National Day of Belgium is celebrated with a large French-Flemish bilingual concert and thousands of litres of beer on Place Jeu de Balles

In 1830, right where the pavé of the square is located, the Renard locomotive factory was built. Business was not good and the factory failed. In 1859, the ground of the former factory was divided into two parts: the first was used to build a barracks for firefighters, the second as a space where the inhabitants of the neighbourhood could play a game called "Balle pelote[14]". A church was also built and became part of the convent of the Capuchin Friars.

Starting in 1873, vendors began to set up on the square, giving rise to what has now become the city's most famous flea market. Open 7 days a week from 6 a.m. until

---

[14] The Balle pelote is a team sport between two teams of five players on a called ground ballodrome. It is a game of gain-ground which takes place in the part West of Belgium, in the provinces of the Walloon Brabant, the Hainaut, Namur and in the western part of Flanders, but also in France, in the valley of Sambre and the Inhabitant of Valenciennes.

2 p.m., it welcomes around 300 vendors of antiques, books, vintage clothes, African masks and various gussets. For collectors of beer glasses, it is not uncommon to find some interesting pieces.

A curiosity is that the square is known by different names: in Flemish is called Vossenplein (Foxes Place, not a tribute to the animals but to the locomotive factory), others call it "Place du Vieux-Marché and others Vlooienmarkt (flat of the flea market).

On the corner of the square and the Rue du Chevreuil, you can admire the building of the "Baths of Brussels" (now called Piscine du Centre), a 5-floor building built in 1949 by the architect Van Nieuwenhuyse with an Art Deco pool.

Below the square, there is still an anti-aircraft shelter, built in 1942, and with an area of about 200 square meters. One of the entrances is still visible in front of the church. It was supposed to be destroyed in 2018 to build an underground car park, but an extraordinary mobilisation of the neighbourhood's inhabitants and vendors blocked the project while preserving the charm of one of the most authentic places in Brussels.

Your beer tour starts from "**Le Brocante**", one of the most fascinating "Lambic café" in the city. In 2019 it was taken over by Sebastien, the current owner, who had worked on site for 15 years as a waiter. If the weather allows, sit at the tables outside and order a classic Gueuze Cantillon along with a tasty Croque Madame listening the music of a gypsy group and watch people go to the market.

From "Le Brocante", take the picturesque Rue de Renards. You will pass in front of the famous Restobieres (at the moment closed but destined to reopen in 2023). Turn left onto Rue Haute, the backbone of the Marolles district.

Marolles is the most authentic neighbourhood in Brussels. From the Chapelle church to the Palais de Justice you can still breathe the authentic Brussels atmosphere with antique shops, street art, art galleries, old cafes and restaurants.

From Rue Haute turn left onto Rue Notre Dame De Graces. You will find yourself in front of the elevator that leads, with no charge, to the Place Poelaert in front of the Palace of Justice, where you can admire a magnificent panoramic view of the city.

It is time to continue your beer tour. From the elevator, take the left and take Rue de Mimimes, where at number 60 you will find the **Cafe des Mimimes**.

This is a trendy bar that has specialised in offering local and seasonal products to its customers. The beer map is characterised by the presence of several local microbreweries. Order a L'Épervier from Brasserie La Source.

From the Café des Mimimes continue straight on the Rue des Mimimes until you reach Place Grand Sablon.

Place Grand Sablon is a triangular square and is the heart of the Sablon district. Every weekend, there is an antiques market. It is surrounded by elegant Maison de maître from the 17th and 18th centuries, while in the centre there is the Minerva fountain (1751), donated by Lord Bruce, Count of Aylesbury, to thank the city that had hosted him.

The square is dominated by the beautiful façade of the church of Notre Dame du Sablon, a masterpiece of Brabant Gothic architecture. Across the tram tracks, there is the Place Petit Sablon, a beautiful, small and delightful "Italian" garden of 1890. The garden is entered through a wrought iron gate. You will see the front of the neoclassical Palazzo Egmont (a building of the Ministry of Foreign Affairs) with its park also open to the public.

From Place Grand Sablon, take Rue Joseph Stevens, and go to number 26 where the **Pistolet Original** deserves a short stop. It is one of the two places in the city (the other is the Restaurant Les Brigittines) where you can drink a Chouke (It consists of equal parts 1-, 2-, and 3-year-old lambics with the entirety of the 2-year component being lambic aged in Armagnac barrels) that I recommend to pair with the Zenne Pistolet Cantillon, a Brussels hot-dog.

From Pistolet, go back to Grand Sablon and take the Rue de Rollebeek which then becomes Rue des Alexiens, cross the junction and stop at number 55 where one of the historic premises of Brussels is located, **La Fleur en Papier Dorè** but unfortunately it has recently closed.

This estaminet was the headquarters of the Belgian surrealist movement in the 1920s. Figures such as painters René Magritte, Pierre Alechinsky, Louis Scutenaire, cartoonist Hergé (creator of Tintin) and songwriter Jacques Brel used this as a meeting place to taste a good Gueuze.

A few metres further on at number 67, you will find **La Porte Noire**, one of the most underrated bars in all of Brussels. Go through the gate and go down the brick stairs. You will find yourself in a cellar that once was the cellar of the convent of the Alexien friars and which today is a beautiful bar with an impressive choice of beers and whiskey.

The atmosphere is halfway between Celtic and medieval. It's not uncommon to watch live music there, usually rock bands. You will have also an impressive choice of beers. I suggest you start with a toasted Adelardus Brune from the Kerkom brewery and enjoy the atmosphere. You are in of one of the best places in Brussels to enjoy a nice evening.

Do not miss:

La Brocante

Rue Blaes 170, 1000 Brussels
Mon — Thu 11-20 Fri — Sun 11-22
5 taps, 100+ bottled beers, restaurant.

Café des Mimimes

Rue des Minimes 60, 1000 Brussels
Mon closed Tue — Sat 12-23.30 Sun 11-16
6 taps, 20+ bottled beers, restaurant.

Pistolet Original

See restaurants page 279.

La Porte Noire

Rue des Alexiens 67, 1000 Brussels
Mon — Thu 17-01 Fri — Sat 17-03 Sun closed
9 taps, 150+ bottled beers, snacks.

Other suggestions:

Mazette

See breweries page 94.

Chaff

Pl. du Jeu de Balle 21/22, 1000 Brussels
Mon 18-01 Mar — Wed 8.30-22 Thu — Sat 8.30-01 Sun
8.30-17
6 taps, 18+ bottled beers, restaurant.

Bistrot in Place Jeu de Balle. It regularly hosts concerts
and DJ sets.

Volle Broll

Pl. du Jeu de Balle 29, 1000 Brussels
Mon — Sun 8-23
5 taps, 20+ bottled beers, snacks.

Typical Brussels estaminet. Very much loved by the
inhabitants of the neighbourhood.

La Clef d'Or

Pl. du Jeu de Balle 1, 1000 Brussels
Mon closed Tue — Sun 06-17
6 taps, 20+ bottled beers, catering.

Another great classic of the Place Jeu de Balles.

Wiel's Renard Noir

Rue Haute 233, 1000 Brussels
Wed — Sun 10-03 Mar 10-00.30
6 taps, 10+ bottled beers, catering.

Historical estaminet of Rue Haute.

Ploegmans

See restaurants page 279.

Les Brigittines

See restaurants page 279.

Au Stekerlapatte

See restaurants page 279.

Gare du Midi – Anderlecht

Brussels-Midi station, more commonly called Gare du Midi, is the most important railway station in Belgium.

Its origins date back to 1840, when it was called Gare des Bogards. At the time, it was nothing more than a wooden building, located in the current Place Rouppe, which served as a terminus to the railway line connecting Brussels to Mons and the French border.

The success of the train as a means of transport soon overwhelmed the Gare des Bogards. Moreover, the location so close to the city centre was problematic. As a result, it was decided to build a larger station in the current location. The monumental building was designed by architect Auguste Payen and opened in 1869.

Over the years, the station has undergone several changes. Most of the modernist buildings were built between 1939 and 1954. The most recent terminal, the one for high-speed trains connecting Brussels to London, Paris, Amsterdam and Cologne, was built in 1992.

Today, it has more than 60,000 passengers per day.

The neighbourhoods around it have also experienced great changes. The area around the Gare du Midi is not among the most recommended in the city and, as around every large station, you need to be attentive, especially in the evening.

If you are passing, departing or arriving from Charleroi Airport (outside the station there is the shuttle bus terminus connecting Brussels to the airport) or waiting for a train, there are some interesting places to sip a good Belgian beer.

The most immediate is the **Taverne Horta**. Among the slew of bars and restaurants just outside the Gare du Midi is undoubtedly the one with the best choice of beer and aesthetically the best furnished. They usually have the Brusge Zot on tap and a good choice of bottled beers.

The area around the Gare du Midi is home to some of the city's most interesting breweries so it's worth spending time anyway.

The most famous is undoubtedly **Cantillon**. To get there, take Avenue Paul-Henry Spaak (where there is the De Lijn bus terminal), then cross Place Bara and continue straight into Rue Limmander and then Rue Gheude. Keeping in mind the opening hours, you can taste unique bottles (not even on sale at the brewery) directly at the brewery, just 10 minutes' walk from the station.

With a classic like Cantillon, I recommend combining one of the new developing breweries of the Brussels beer scene; the **Brasserie de l'Ermitage**. From Cantillon, follow Rue Gheude towards the station and then turn on the street that turns left, Rue Lambert Crickx. At number 26, you will find the brewery with an adjoining tap room where you can quench your thirst with a Noire du Midi.

And if you are still thirsty (and you have still time) with a 15-minute walk from Gare du Midi you can reach

Brasserie de la Jungle. Walk along Rue Bara and then turn right onto Rue des Deux Gare where on the right you will find one of the city's most recent micro-breweries and quench your thirst with a Jungle Saison.

Do not miss:

Taverne Horta

PL. Victor Horta 30, 1060 Saint-Gilles
Mon — Fri 6-22 Sat — Sun closed
6 taps, 10+ bottled beers, restaurant.

Chapeau Blanc

Rue Wayez 200, 1070 Anderlecht
3 taps, 20 bottled beers, restaurant.

A classic Belgian bistrot, one of the last Flemish bars of Brussels. Good choice of beer and classic disches.

Brassserie Cantillon

See breweries page 29.

Brasserie de l'Ermitage

See breweries page 60.

Brasserie de la Jungle

See breweries page 77.

Other suggestions:

Les Caves de l'Ermitage

See beershop page 267.

St. Gilles

Saint-Gilles is a municipality located in central south of Brussels. It is a multicultural place with a very bohemian atmosphere that attracts musicians, artists, poets and writers.

St. Gilles is a true ethnic and cultural melting pot. Over the years the historic Portuguese and Spanish communities have been flanked by a large Maghreb and African component. In recent years, the municipality has seen the arrival of a growing Italian community.

St. Gilles is highly regarded from an architectural point of view thanks to its numerous Art Deco and Art Nouveau buildings. There are bars and restaurants of all kinds and it is one of the richest areas, from the beer point of view, of the city. Its beating heart is the famous "Parvis de Saint-Gilles", easily accessible from all parts of the city thanks to the pre-metro station.

Your tour starts right here, more precisely at **Café Maison du Peuple**. Opened in 2008, it has carved out an important existence in the "Parvis" next to historic bars such as the Brasserie de l'Union and the Brasserie Verschure, and has become one of the landmarks of the nightlife not only in St. Gilles but of all Brussels.

There is a fine terrace on the Parvis, and spacious interiors with brick walls. The bar is always crowded, and in the evenings it is quite common to come across live music or DJ sets. This tour in the heart of St. Gilles will be quiet long, so why not order a Zinnebir from Brasserie de la Senne?

From Café Maison du Peuple, turn to the corner of Parvis, and the historic **Brasserie de l'Union**.

It is a real institution of the city. It is a charming old estaminet, always full, dedicated to one of the city's historic teams; The Royal Union Saint-Gilloise.

Even here it is quite common during the evening to come across live music and in a very bohemian atmosphere. Order a Saison de Bruxelles from the local brewery L'Annexe.

Retrace your steps and towards the church on the Parvis. At the opposite end of the Brasserie de l'Union, there is another historic place in Saint Gilles; the **Brasserie Verschuren** in pure art-deco style. During the Covid pandemic it seemed to be on the brink of failure but managed to survive thanks to a combination of crowdfunding (with around EUR 17,000 raised in two weeks) and a regional loan. In addition, thanks to the momentum of the support received, the owner, Robert Van Craen, announced that he has purchased the famous restaurant Restobières closed since May 2021 which will reopen in 2023 after the necessary renovations.

Take a closer look at the architecture of the building while sipping a Verschueren Triple (brewed for them by Brasserie de la Senne); an art-nouveau/deco glass ceiling on the entrance porch, carved wood and arches celebrate the craftsmanship of another time.

From the Brasserie Verschuren, continue on the Chausse de Waterloo. In a 15-minute walk you will be at the **Dynamo Bar**.

The Dynamo Bar is one of the most interesting and "revolutionary" novelties to the Brussel beer scene.

"Revolutionary" because it was the first bar, together with Le Barboteur in Schaerbeek, to devote itself exclusively to the "craft" beer scene and to put traditional Belgian beers in the background. "Interesting" because at Dynamo you can find the best craft beers of the moment from all over Europe.

Look at the wooden board where draught beers are shown and order a Porter from a British brewery, a style that it is not easy to find at these latitudes.

From Dynamo, take Rue Antoine Bréart and then turn left onto Rue Arthur Diderich. At the junction on the left you will find the **Moeder Lambic Original**, the best place to close the evening in the area.

The name Chez Moeder Lambic has a long history in Brussels dating back to the early 20th century. At the time there was an estaminet of the same name located in the Bois de la Cambre region in Brussels. This region was far from the hectic city of Brussels and many residents went to this area of the "urban park" to relax and get away from the city. On the edge of the park, there was the maison de bière, Chez Moeder Lambic. Photographs, postcards and references exist from the early 1900s up until the 1950s. According to Hervé Gérard, the building that housed Moeder Lambic was built in 1672 and was frequented by famous people like Lord Byron and Sir Walter Scott. The building was razed to the ground in 1975.

The current Moeder Lambic was taken over in 2006 by Jean Hummler and Nassim Dessicy. At the time, they were working there as bartenders and when the old owner went to bankrupt, they decided to buy it. Jean and Nassim revolutionised the beer scene in Brussels by closing the door of their restaurant to all industry-related beer products. The success led them to open a second location in the centre with a new partner, Andy Mengal.

The original is always better than the copy. And in my opinion it also applies to the Moeder Lambic. The place is still authentic and with a very professional staff always ready to advise you. In addition, it is much less chaotic than the Moeder Lambic in the city centre. It consists of a not so big room at the ground floor and in a kind of cave.

Here, I advise you to ask for the menu of the bottles and order a Vermeesch, a new very interesting spontaneous fermentation producer.

Do not miss:

Café Maison du Peuple

Parv. de Saint-Gilles 39, 1060 Saint-Gilles
Sun — Thu 9.30-00 Fri — Sat 9.30-03
8 taps, 10+ bottled beers, restaurant.

Brasserie de l'Union

Parv. de Saint-Gilles 55, 1060 Saint-Gilles
Mon — Wed 08-01
Thu — Sun 08-1.30
8 taps, 30+ bottled beers, restaurant.

Brasserie Verschuren

Parv. de Saint-Gilles 11, 1060 Saint-Gilles
Mon — Sun 08-01
1 tap, 20+ bottled beers, catering.

Dynamo Bar

Chau. d'Alsemberg 130, 1060 Saint-Gilles
Sun — Wed 17-00 Thu — Sat 17-01
18 taps, 150+ bottled beers, snacks.

Moeder Lambic Original

Rue de Savoie, 68-1060 Saint-Gilles
Mon — Thu 16-00 Fri 16-01 Sat 14-01 Sun 14-00

Other suggestions:

Le Dillens

PL. Julien Dillens 11, 1060 Saint-Gilles
Mon — Thu 08-00 Fri 08-01 Sat 10-01 Sun 10-00
6 taps, 25+ bottled beers, catering.

Historic and well-known bar-bistro of Saint Gilles. Excellent selection of beers, mainly from Brussels, and the possibility to taste different types of Cantillon 0.75.

L'Ermitage Saint-Gilles

Rue de Moscou 34, 1060 Saint-Gilles
Mon — Sun 16-01
It is the real tap room of Brasserie de l'Ermitage. Possibility to have lunch or dinner on site with pizzas cooked on site. See breweries page

Brasserie Egalitè

Parv. de Saint-Gilles 47, 1060 Saint-Gilles
Mon — Sun 08-02
+ 500 bottled beers

Good option with a large choice of beer.

L'Annexe

See breweries page 66.

Chez mon ex

Rue de Roumanie 2, 1060 Saint-Gilles
Mon — Sat 15-00
6 taps, 15+ bottled beers, restaurant.

Fashionable place with a limited but good choice of beers.

L'Amère a boire Saint-Gilles

AV. Paul Dejaer 20, 1060 Saint-Gilles
Mon — Sun 16-01

Sister bar of the one near Place Flagey. Very good choice
of beers.

Dynamo - Cave de Soif

See berstore page 265.

Beerstorming

See breweries page 69.

Bar du Matin

Chau. d'Alsemberg 172, 1190 Forest
Mon — Thu 08-01 Fri — Sat 09-03 Sun 09-01
6 taps, 15+ bottled beers, restaurant.

Located on the border between the municipalities of Forest and Saint Gilles and just outside the Albert premetro exit. During the day it is frequented by locals and students, at night it comes alive with DJs and live music.

Malt Attacks

See beer shop page 265.

Liesse

See restaurants page 279.

La Porteuse d'Eau

AV. Jean Volders 48, 1060 Saint-Gilles
Tue — Sun 11-23.30 Mon closed
3 taps, 30+ bottles, restaurant

Located in a beautiful building built by architect Ernest Blerot in pure Art nouveau style. Apart from the Trappists, the choice of beers is not exceptional, but it is worth having a drink to admire the interiors and beautiful stained glass windows.

Addict Bar

Chaussee de Waterloo 327, 1060 Sint-Gilles
Mon – Wed 09-01 Thu – Fri 09-03 Sat 12-03 Sun 12-00
7 taps, +70 bottles, snacks.

The Jupiler sign outside wouldn't exactly lure us in. However, like so many bars in Belgium, Addict Bar has a contractual obligation to serve some InBev beers. The beer board is bursting with local beers, and beers from other independent breweries in Belgium.

La Biche

PL. Maurice van Meenen 1, 1060 Saint-Gilles
Mon — Thu — Sun 8.30-00 Fri — Sat 9.30-01
6 taps, 20+ bottles, snacks

Corner bar with good choice of local beers.

La Bagarre

Rue de Tamines 2, 1060 Saint-Gilles
Tue – Thu 17-00 Fri – Sat 17-01 Sun – Mon closed
10 taps, + 20 cans, food.

One of the most pleasant additions during 2024 is the tap room of the brewery DrinkThatBeer (part of Co-Hop). In addition to their beers, you can find other Co-Hop branded products.

Focus: Moeder Lambic

You can't write a book about beer in Brussels without talking to those who created one of the symbols of the beer scene in the city. Jean Hummler is French but has Belgian beer in his veins. He made the Moeder Lambic the outpost of craft beers in Brussels and made it one of the meccas of world beer tourism.

In a period of great changes, I thought that a chat with him could be useful to understand the beer scene of the city and to understand how the famous Moeder Lambic will change in the coming years.

Interview with Jean Hummler:

How and when did your adventure begin?

In 2004, I was working here at Moeder Lambic in St. Gilles as a bartender. The philosophy of the bar was completely different. There were 8-9 taps with Belgian and foreign industrial beers and about 300 bottled beers, there was a bit of everything. The owner of the bar went bankrupt and along with my current partner, Nassim, who was also a bartender, we took over the place.

The first thing we did was to terminate all sorts of supply agreements with industrial groups like Duvel Moortgat, Chimay Trappist, or Lambic manufacturers who used sweeteners like Lindeamans and Mort Subite. We also removed from the menu sodas and industrial cheeses.

We were the pioneers of craft beers in Brussels and for a long time the only craft beer bar in the city. We were among the first to work with Brasserie de la Senne, among the first to serve the iconic Taras Boulba.

At the time, talking about Lambic and excluding Cantillon, Brussels was a desert. We were the first to serve Lambic from the pump, to produce traditional Faro.

In 2009, we were still the only ones, although someone else had started serving craft beer. That year, we decided to open a new place in the city centre, the place that today is the Moeder Lambic Fontanas.

The adventure in the city centre was not easy. The first two years in particular were very difficult. The customers, locals and tourists, expected the classic industrial beers. We offered craft beers, we were ahead of the market. With a lot of work, and a little luck, we survived.

2015 was the year of acceleration. Then, there were so many events and changes: the terrorist attacks in Brussels, the pedestrianisation of the city centre and finally the COVID pandemic, which changed everything.

How has the COVID pandemic changed or will it change your business?

Many beer bars have closed or are destined to do so. The market right now is favourable to tap rooms and brewpubs. Even a brewery with modest beers if it has a tap room is trendy now. People want to taste new products, preferably in cans and with nice labels.

We need to evolve and change. We have abolished table service. People complained about the prices of beers but we were the only ones to offer this kind of product.

Now, we'll split the two bars. The Moeder Lambic in St. Gilles will remain a local bar, already 95 % of our customers are from the neighbourhood.

In the city centre, we will start producing Dry Mead, Lemonade and Kombucha in collaboration with Brasserie H20. We will become a brewpub. In the future, we will also produce cider and we would like to have barrels to age Lambic. We will start production at the end of 2022 in order to be ready in 2023.

We have served beers from all over the world for years, but now we will work more with the local breweries. It'll be different.

Activities like Tap Takeover are over. Consumers are now buying beers online. The market has changed.

We have also tried to reduce prices but we will be forced to raise them due to the energy crisis.

During Covid, we lost 90 % of our staff. It is not easy to work in the HoReCa sector, the conditions are difficult and working hours are demanding. We have trouble finding staff and training them properly.

Everything is getting more expensive. In Belgium, prices have risen a lot compared to 5 years ago. A beer from the other side of the world is too expensive. We should sell it for EUR 10/12 and serve 8 cl. We do not want to do this even if there were some of our customers willing to pay these prices.

We will focus on simple and local products. After all, beer is something to drink and the bar is a place to relax and share nice moments with family and friends. It will be a nice change because at Moeder Lambic we have people coming from all over the world and contacts everywhere.

When Leonardo Di Vincenzo sold Birra del Borgo to the industry, together with bars like Ma che Siete Venuti in Fa' in Roma and Akkurat in Stockholm we decided to react. We have not allowed the industry to penetrate this world.

Everything is going too fast, it is impossible to follow the beer market.

I talked to Manuele Colonna of Ma che Siete Venuti in Fa' and he told me he dreams to have a place with only two beers: a Keller from Franconia and a Lambic of Belgium. With a TV to watch games. New breweries are opened and new beers are born everywhere. And people always expect novelties.

All craft beer bars will have to change their approach. Some will become restaurants, others brewpubs. COVID has changed everything and the crisis will make things worse.

Lambic producers are popping up like mushrooms, what do you think about this phenomenon?

In Belgium, we did everything with Lambic in the past, we have done the worst. New producers are part of the rebirth. Vermeesch, Bokke, Bofkont, Lambiek Fabrik, Deville…they have all clear ideas. The Brussels Beer Project has hired important brewers to entrust them with the production of Lambic.

The new actors focus a lot on quality. They're passionate people. Each actor has his own way of blending, bringing a new interpretation. We'll have a lot more choice and that's a good thing.

Prices will remain high. Lambic was a cheap drink. Today it is no longer cheap.

How do you think the Brussels beer scene will evolve in the coming years?

The beer market in Brussels is worth about one million hectolitres per year. It is a high consumption, thanks also to the large number of tourists. In the craft beer world there are two great players; the Brasserie de la Senne and the Brussels Beer Project that together make more or less 20000 hectolitres. The other producers together reach a maximum of 60000. So, they cover a quota ranging from 5 to 10 % of the beer drunk in Brussels. The rest is all industrial beer. Therefore, there is still room to expand.

But for breweries that only focus on beer production, there is no room left. En Stomelings who had this focus is changing. The others are almost all brewpubs, or have a tap room.

BBP and De la Senne also have bars.

Having a Tap room is now fundamental, you sell directly without any intermediary and therefore you have much higher margins.

This means the death of beer bars. We ourselves are the best customers of breweries that have become our competitors.

How did the idea of the BXL Beer Fest come about?

I created it together with Kevin Desmet and Olivier Desmet of Nüetnigenough in 2017.

We wanted a different festival, to always serve beers in clean glasses and of course have only craft breweries. To offer a fresh image of Brussels and its beers.

Usually, we have a mix of Belgian breweries and foreign breweries. We invite those foreign breweries because they love Belgian beers. They realise that there is no market for them here. We aim to have between 8000 and 9000 visitors. But not more because we want to maintain a human dimension in which it is possible to interact with the brewers, create connections and bonds.

What's your favourite beer?

The XX Bitter by De Ranke

And your favourite beer from a Brussels brewery?

Cantillon's Lambic, but I love all their beers. It's hard to choose.

Focus: Dynamo Bar

For years Dynamo Bar has been a reference point for lovers of the boundless craft beer scene. Countless tap takeovers, a Festival (the SWAFF) and a list of beers full of taste from all over Europe.

With Greg, I discussed the future of craft beer bars in Brussels and much more.

Interview with Grégoire Rifaut:

How and when did your adventure begin?

We opened on October 29, 2015. I had the idea in mind since April 2014. I had lived and worked in London and I didn't like the beers on offer in Brussels. I've always loved the way the British go to the bar. I wanted to export a model, do something different. Between the idea and its realisation some time has passed, 15 months to be precise.

What is the philosophy behind of Dynamo Bar?

When you enter the bar, you are immediately in front of the counter, a counter that occupies about half of the room because I want to encourage interaction between those behind the counter and the customer. My idea is that there should be a maximum of 5 meters between the client and the bartender.

I chose a corner bar for light and because I wanted a place where there were many doors to enter and leave. I want to offer many different beer styles from all over the Europe and the World. Of course, just craft beers. Our tap list is always very balanced to offer beers for all tastes. However, a place is always reserved for lesser-known beer styles in Belgium such as mild, bitter etc.

We are not just a beer geek bar. Otherwise, we would have already closed because that customer base is limited and the offer for them in recent years has expanded.

Our target is those people who love beers and who mainly reside in this neighbourhood.

What kind of activities do you organise?

We organise several tap takeovers but less than in the past. Let's say that by now we organise them for pleasure, with breweries we value. You do not earn from an economic point of view and you need to overturn the menu, making some customers dissatisfied.

We were organising homebrewers night. Before Covid, it worked. Homebrewers number have decreased and they now meet on their own. They no longer need to convene. With the increased supply of beer, homebrewing is in decline. In the US, they are already talking of this phenomenon. Beer enthusiast have more choice and are less tempted to brew beer on their own.

How did the idea of the SWAFF Beer Festival come about?

The idea came from Sebastien of Barboteur and Antoine of Malt Attack. Antoine proposed that I join. I was curious and so I joined. I am more nerdy, Seb more enthusiastic and motivated, Antoine quieter. We had a good balance. For three years, we organised everything together. Post COVID, people reflect more about what they like in life, Antoine preferred to take himself out.

The last edition was just me and Seb. We also had to change locations because the municipality of Molenbeek no longer wanted to allow us use of Karreveld Castle. It was not easy to find a location like that, with probably the best outdoor courtyard in Brussels.

The new location (La Vallèe — an atelier also located in Molenbeek) has potential, but I'm not sure that we have fully exploited it. Most likely, next year the Festival will take place on Friday evenings and Saturdays and no longer on Sunday. We'll have more live music.

How has the COVID pandemic changed, or how will it change your business?

We risk disappearing. When we opened, I thought; we are the future. I was wrong. If you analyse how many 100 % craft beer bars have opened you will see that there are few.

Breweries have increased, especially those with tap rooms or brewpubs. We are an exception in Europe, Brussels has more breweries than craft beer pubs.

On the other hand, if you open a craft beer pub, you do not make money. If you open a brewery you have tax breaks, subsidised loans and donations from customers. If I would go back, I would open a Brewpub. It takes more money but they lend you more money.

Is this an added value for the Brussels brewery scene? I don't think so. We offer things that they don't offer. But the customer always decides. And at this stage, customers find it more beneficial to go directly to the source for the fresh product. That's why at Dynamo we target people in our area who like to relax and have fun and try to introduce them to new beers.

How do you think the Brussels beer scene will evolve in the coming years?

I don't have an answer. I think there's still room for more breweries. It all depends on external factors. As long as the customer is willing to pay more for a beer, there will be room. If there is a crisis that will lead to a reduction of economies of scale, everything will change.

There is a part of the community that loves craft beers that is willing to pay more and more for beers. Therefore, if one makes good products and has a good image it could have success.

Seventeen/eighteen breweries is still a sustainable number. To predict what will happen in Brussels, you have to go to London or Paris. In Paris, I saw a night shop selling North Brewing beers. The night shop we have in front at the moment sells BBP's Delta IPA and Brasserie de la Senne beers. Five years ago, it didn't sell them. That's why I think there's still room.

What's your favourite beer?

Export Porter by The Kernel. A beer I could drink in any situation.

And your favourite beer from a Brussels brewery?

I'd say Zinne Pils. It's a much underrated beer, it's the one that really changed the scene in Brussels. It is the beer that allowed craft beers to compete with the beers produced by industrial breweries. Without Zenne Pils, probably here at Dynamo we would never have served Pils.

Where to drink in the rest of the city

In the previous chapters, we visited premises in the most central municipalities easy reachable by those who are on holiday or visiting Brussels.

However, there are some hidden gems in area less beaten by beer hunters.

In Den Achtsten Hemel

PL. Peter Benoit 1, 1120 Brussels
Mon — Sat 11-21 Dom closed

It is a real gem, outside of any tourist circuit. It is a cafe-bistro located a short distance from the Brussels Ring. Here the story has stopped and the restaurant has the best selection of Lambic in all of Brussels. To reach it from the city centre, take tram number 3 (direction Esplanade) to Heembeek station and then bus 47 (direction Vilvoorde) to Peter Benoit stop.

Beergium Bar

Chau. de Waterloo 1227, 1180 Uccle
Wed 17.30-23 Thu — Fri 17.30-00 Sat 16.30-00 Sun 16.30-23

The Beergium is definitely the "place to be" for drinking beer in the commune of Uccle. Located rather outside the centre, the ideal way to reach it is to take the efficient network of local trains that connect the various areas of the city and the municipalities of the hinterland, and get off at the stop Diesdelle/Vivier D'Oie.

The Beergium Bar opened in July 2019 and is a branch of the beer distributor Beergium, founded by Sébastien Caucheteur and Fanny Delhaye and based in the locality of Le Roeulx in Wallonia. They sell beers from all over the world.

The Beergium's 25-tap system with Belgian and foreign beers (mostly American) is a true paradise for beer geeks. There is an electronic panel that shows the Untapped rating of draught beers and a very good selection of bottled beers.

Au Vieux Spijtigen Duivel

Chau. d'Alsemberg 621, 1180 Uccle
Mon — Sun 11.30-00
5 taps, 40+ bottled beers, restaurant.

A historic brasserie frequented by Charles Baudelaire and Victor Hugo. It is now owned by a Greek. Average food but excellent and varied choice of beers.

Silex Bar

Rue Middelbourg 124, 1170 Watermael-Boitsfort
Wed – Fri 16 – 23 Sat – Sun 12 – 23

The most recent novelty in the beer bar scene of the city. It is located in Watermael-Boitsfort, quite far from the city center. There are beers from Brussels breweries DrinkDrink! And La Source on tap.

Dekkera

Rue Pierre Decoster 109, 1190 Forest
Tue — Sun 15-23 Mon closed

Located in the municipality of Forest, in the southwest part of the city. It is a real neighbourhood bar (with 5 taps with rotating beers) that also serves as a beer shop. It offers about 170 beers, all of Belgian craft breweries. The name recalls the yeast Dekkera Bruxellensis present in Lambic.

Houblons de Brussels

Rue du Bois 1, 1090 Jette

A "Houblonniere" (a "hop factory") located near the forest of Laerbeek, on the border between the municipalities of Jette and Ganshoren. It is a true green oasis nestled between the highway and the railway.

The idea of the founder, Christophe Speltiens, is to bring hops cultivation back to Brussels. Hops were once grown around Brussels in the area between the cities of Asse and Aalst, but now confined to Poperinge in East Flanders. The soil and the area are ideal due to the fact that there is a microclimate, less wind, and a temperature about two degrees higher than the surrounding areas.

They are experimenting with the cultivation of Belgian, German, British and American hops, preferring aromatic varieties over bitter ones.

At the same time, as part of the crowdfunding campaign to support this project, Christophe Speltiens created recipes for two beers, Super Deluxe and Hoppy Bunny, which were initially produced at the Valduc-Thor brewery in Wallonia, and now in Brussels at Brasserie En Stomelings.

He has also established collaboration with Cantillon, planting rows of the Coigneau hops, once highly valued by Lambic producers due to the low degree of amertume, and for the great spread in the area. But for the Cantillon blend with Coigneau, it will take a few more years.

Houblons de Bruxelles organises guided tours and tastings, usually on weekends. It can be a good option for a different kind of trip, in an environment totally different from that of the city.

De Gele Poraa

Rue Jules Lahaye 27, 1090 Jette
Sun — Thu 18-01 Fri — Sat 18-03
1 tap, 30+ bottled beers, snacks.

A student bar located in the municipality of Jette, outside the tourist circuits of Brussels. Beers with very competitive prices, pool and table football available.

Excelsior Stam

Rue de l'Eglise Saint-Pierre 8, 1090 Jette
Sun – Thu 16-01 Fri – Sat 16-03 Mon closed
2 taps, +100 bottles, snacks

A neighbourhood bar with a pleasant atmosphere, good choice of beers (with a focus on different Brussels breweries), table football and theme nights.

La Cave à Bière

AV. Georges Henri 193, 1200 Woluwe-Saint-Lambert
Mon — Sun 08-01
If you are in the residential municipality of Woluwe-Saint-Lambert, La Cuve à Bière is worth a stop. The interior is of a classic Brussels estaminet and with good

choice of craft beer alongside the ubiquitous industrial beers that dominate the bars of these areas of the city.

La Rose Blanche

Chau. de Merchtem 53, 1080 Molenbeek-Saint-Jean
Mon — Sun 9.30-22.30

Opened in 1973 and run by the brothers Pavlos and Kostas Karassavidis, this is a real living monument, serving the last Greek coffee in the municipality of Molenbeek.

Molenbeek, which has always been a receptacle of waves of emigration (Italian and Greek before, Turkish and North African now) is one of the most problematic areas of the city, sadly known in news items due to terror attacks that have recently hit Europe.

The Rose Blanche is a clear example of how integration is possible, being frequented by Greeks, Arabs, Turks and Belgians without any issues of any kind.

The bar has been at risk of closure several times. Today, it is protected by an association, the "Amicale de la Rose Blanche" and a book and a film have been dedicated to it.

It is one of the few bars serving alcohol in Molenbeek. Don't expect craft beers or lambic, but a visit is definitely worth the experience!

Where to drink in Brussels Parks

What's better than drinking a good craft beer in the middle of nature?

Brussels, as the real Beer capital, weather permitting and during spring and the summer, also offers this.

The Brussels-Capital Region has a nature heritage of exceptional extent; 1,700 hectares of forest (the Forêt de Soignes) and 600 hectares of municipal parks and gardens scattered throughout the city. Brussels has the highest ratio of green area per capita of all European capitals (about 30 square meters per inhabitant), which is why it can boast of the title of European city with most green spaces.

The city is a very environmentally friendly, as demonstrated by the care of numerous public parks and wonderful gardens, traffic control, and other initiatives to support ecological mobility. The richness and beauty of the green areas encourages you to take long and pleasant walks, to spend a few hours of relaxation in the shade of a tree, to discover the city by bike or on foot, allowing yourself be enchanted by the scents and colours of nature.

From May to September, there are several kiosks opened in the different parks of the city. In some cases, they are real bars. The choice of beer is not very wide but almost everywhere you can find interesting products.

Keep in mind that every year these bars must apply for the renewal of the concession, so it is not certain that the premises you will find listed here are still in business.

Park Elisabeth, Koekelberg

The Park Elisabeth extends from the immense Basilica of the Sacred Heart of Koekelberg to the Botanique Gardens. Koekelberg Basilica is the largest Art Deco building in the world with its 89 meters high and 167 meters long.

Bar Eliza

This is the only real beer attraction in the municipality of Koekelberg (rather arid when it comes to beer) in addition to the newborn Tipsy Tribe brewery. It is a wooden cabin with the possibility of eating on site. Usually, they organise musical and cultural activities. To go there, take the metro to Simonis station.

Bois de la Cambre

The Bois de la Cambre is the green lung of Brussels. It is located at the end of the Avenue Louise and is the extension into the city of the Forêt of Soignes. It is the most visited park in the city, ideal for long walks, bikes, and for jogging or organising picnics. Inside, it has an artificial lake where you can rent pedal boats and small boats to reach the Chalet Robinson, a very trendy restaurant located on the islet in the middle of the lake. The Bois de la Cambre offers several options including restaurants (Brasserie Patinoire, with adjoining ballroom) and bars.

Woodpecker

Probably the most interesting place, and where you can taste the beers of Brasserie de la Senne and taste the gourmet dishes of Gregory Marlier (of the Bia Mara restaurant) and the exquisite chocolate creations of the

Maître chocolatier Laurent Gerbaud, and with live music and DJ sets.

Le Kiosque

A simple kiosk opens all year round. Snacks and beers from Vedett and Ciders by Ruwet available.

La Flore

Beautiful location deep in the forest. It is a more sophisticated place than the others in Bois de la Cambre. Chouffe blonde, Delta IPA (BBP) and Triple Karmeliet as a choice of beers.

Jardin Cambre

Located in front of the famous "Les Jeux d'Hiver" in the heart of Bois de la Cambre. Interesting Bobby Brewery beers on the menu.

Parc du Cinquantenaire

The Parc du Cinquantenaire was built thanks to King Leopold II in 1880, to celebrate the 50th anniversary of Belgian independence. It is probably the most famous urban park in Brussels. It extends in the eastern part of the European Quarter over an area of about 30 hectares. In addition to paths, gardens and hedges there are buildings, monuments and works of art. Among those are worth mentioning; the Horta-Lambeaux Pavilion that encloses "Human Passions", a beautiful marble relief, and the Great Mosque, the Islamic centre of Brussels since 1978.

At the top of the park, there is the classical palace consisting of two wings and hemicycle joined by an arch, erected in 1905, and inspired by the famous triumphal arch in Berlin. The building houses the Museum of Art and History, the Army Museum and the Automobile Museum.

Guinguette Parc du Cinquantenaire — Bar Maurice

A chain of summer bars found in the main parks of Brussels. Interesting choice of beers with products from Brasserie Silly, Dupont, DrinkDrink and BBP.

Park Royale

The Brussels Park, commonly called the Royal Park, extends for 13 hectares over what was once the ancient hunting ground of the Dukes of Brabant and which was then transformed in 1776 into a beautiful French garden. It is the largest urban public park in the centre of Brussels, overlooked by the old building of the Royal Palace, the Belgian Parliament, and along Rue Royale. The park is intersected by large avenues and embellished with carved statues and dancing fountains.

La Guinguette Royale

Same concept and owners of the Woodpecker of Bois de la Cambre.

Park Josaphat

With its 20 hectares, it is the green lung of the populous municipality of Schaerbeek. It is a historical park divided into three parts: the historic park, the large lawn and the play area. It is historically a reserve of writers and artists and shelter of botanists and ornithologists. It houses two bars.

La Laiterie

It was originally a dairy. In the 80's Schaerbeekois used to eat plattekeis tartine and drink a local beer. It is now managed by the owners of the Woodpecker of Bois de la Cambre.

Buvette Sint-Sebastian

It is a real restaurant located in the heart of Parc Josaphat. In addition to excellent cuisine, it offers an excellent choice of beers with Gueuze from Cantillon, Boon and Girardin, the Trappist Orval, the Moinette of Dupont and the beers of Brasserie de la Senne.

Abbaye de la Cambre

The Abbey of La Cambre was a Cistercian monastery in Ixelles, not far from Place Flagey. It was founded in 1201 by Dame Gisele and suppressed in 1796, following the French Revolution. Over the years, it has hosted various military buildings and the National Geographical Institute. Today, it houses the prestigious Ecole Nationale Superiore of Visual Arts. The Abbey has a beautiful garden.

In 2014, the entrepreneur Vincent Poswick launched three beers (blonde, Ambre and Triple) bearing the Abbaye de la Cambre brand. The beers do not bear the mark of abbey beers because they are not brewed on site, but rather by the Brasserie Het Anker of Mechelen.

Guinguette Gisele

Same chain as the Guinnguette of the Parc du Cinquantenaire.

Parc de Laeken

Laeken Park is part of a vast landscape and complex comprising the "Domaine Royal" (possession of the Belgian royal house) and several parks in the north of Brussels (Osseghem, Jardins du Fleuriste, Sobieski, Colonial). It is one of the few examples of a French garden in Belgium with wide avenues and large meadows with parterre of flowers.

From the park you can admire the famous Atomium one of the best know symbols of Brussels. The Atomium is a steel construction that represents the nine atoms of a unit cell of an iron crystal. Designed by architect André Waterkeyn it was built on the occasion of Expo 1958, the historic universal exhibition that changed the face of the city. The original intention was that it would stay on site just for some months, but it has turned out otherwise. Open now to visitors, the spheres are connected by escalators.

Guinguette André

Between a walk in Parc Laeken and a visit to the Atomium, you can stop at the Guinguette André, a twin bar of those already referred to in Parc du Cinquantenaire and the Abbey of la Cambre.

Parc de Forest

Another beautiful urban park of 13 hectares that often hosts concerts and live music. From its highest point, which served as an observation point during the First World War, you can admire a splendid view of Brussels.

Guinguette du Parc du Forest

At the time of writing this book (2022) it was under renovation due to works in the park.

Where to drink at the airport

As you may know, a good beer helps you to sleep during the trip and makes the waiting more pleasant.

Below are some tips where to taste the last (?) beer of your holiday in Brussels.

Brussels Nationale — Zaventem

Assuming that you won't find exceptional beers, at Gate A the "Place to be" is the **Beer&Cheers** while the **Brewgate** is worth a stop at Gate B.

To be fair, I also mention the Leffe Bar and the Jupiler Gate (both at Gate A).

Brussels South Charleroi

The best place, with a nice view on the airway is **The Speakeasy** (Terminal 1). As an alternative, the **Charle's brewing company** (Terminal 1 and 2).

Beer store

Brussels, as the real Beer Capital, also offers to its visitors many specialised shops where one can buy, and in some cases even taste, beers of all kinds.

In this chapter, you will find an overview of the most complete Beershops in the city. Ideal places where you can buy a beer that you particularly liked, or to find some interesting gift opportunities. Some of these beershops also ship abroad.

In general, the prices are still quite affordable, but my advice is to always buy, where possible, at the source (the brewery itself).

Also, keep in mind that in Brussels, and Belgium, craft beers can be easily found in supermarkets. All three major chains (Delhaize, Carrefour and Colruyt) offer local products on their shelves (from De La Senne, Annexe, En Stoemelings, BBP).

Finally, the city has a chain of "Night Shops", mostly run by Indians or Pakistanis, which in many cases offer an interesting selection of beers, often even stored in the fridge and ready to drink.

Beer Mania

Chausse de Wavre 174 — https://beermania.be

The historic Beer Mania is located a stone's throw from the European Institutions district. Opened in 1981, it was the first beer shop in the world to offer an online sales service in 1997. That service continues today with the opportunity to buy beer and receive it in any corner of the globe. Customers are offered almost 500 beers, from all over Belgium at good price. It is equipped with two rooms and a striking terrace, where it is usually possible to taste beers on site and enjoy the classic "frites" or a rich plateau of cheeses.

Malt Attacks

18 Avenue Jean Volders — https://www.maltattacks.com/ Tue — Fri 11-19 Sat 12-18

Located in the picturesque and multi-ethnic municipality of Saint Gilles. It is a beer shop specialising in the sale of beers from foreign breweries (especially English and Scandinavian) and emerging Belgian producers. There are about 600 beers and homebrewing material on offer. You can also fill a takeaway growler with the beers present at the moment on tap.

Dynamo Bar

Chau. d'Alsemberg 130, 1060 Saint-Gilles

Located also in Saint Gilles, in addition to being an excellent bar offers take-away solutions for practically all the bottles for sale at a price Euro 1/1.5 above the menu price. Here too, there one can fill a growler with one of the beers that are on tap at the moment.

Dynamo - Cave de Soif

Rue Africaine 86, 1060 Saint-Gilles

It opened at the end of 2023. You can find all the beers available at Dynamo Bar plus some "whales".

Malting Pot

Rue Scarron 50 - https://www.maltingpot.be/en/home
Tue — Fri 12-19 Sat 12-18

Near the famous Place Flagey, we find Malting Pot. More than 200 beers, mostly Belgian producers are on offer, but with a good presence of foreign breweries (From UK and Scandinavia).

Huens

Adolphe Buyl 3. 1050 Ixelles
Mon — Sun 16-22

Founded in 1917, this is the oldest beer store in the city. Nestled in the university district, it serves the many students of the neighbourhood.

Fermenthinghs

Rue Dieudonné Lefèvre 4 – https://www.fermenthings.be
Wed — Thu — Sat 10-17 Fri 8.30-18.30 Sun 11-15

Located at the Be-Here (together with Brasserie La Source) in the north-east part of the city in what is becoming the "Beer Mile" of Brussels where, a few metres from each other, we find the breweries No Science, La Source, En Stoemelings and Brasserie de la Senne. To label Fermenthings as a "beer shop" is too simple, as it is presented as an actual laboratory dedicated to everything related to fermentation (it often organises courses focused on the topic). The shop, among other things, has a good selection of beers and ciders.

Prik and Tik

Rue Steyls 118, 1020 Brussels
Mon — Fri 9-17 Sat 9-13

Wholesale seller specialised in beverages of all kinds. It has a vast assortment of Belgian and foreign beers (about 500).

Python Bar

Avenue Emile Max 55

The Python Bar opened quite recently (August 2018). It is small but rather welcoming and offers a good choice of local and foreign craft beers.

Barboteur

Avenue Louis Bertrand 23

It offers a good choice of beers from all over the world.

Dekkera

Rue Pierre Decoster 109

In the southwest part of the city, we find the Dekkera. It is a real neighbourhood bar that also serves as a beer shop. About 170 beers, all of Belgian craft breweries, are on offer there.

Beergium

Chaussée de Waterloo 1227 - https://www.beergium.com/

In the southeast, we find the very interesting Beergium, a bar that opened in July 2019 following an e-commerce experience (which is still active). More than a thousand beers are available, including an excellent choice of American products.

La Tana in Brussels

Rue de l'Enseignement 27, 1000 Brussels

Although not really a beer shop (it is a restaurant with Roman cuisine) the restaurant offers an excellent and varied choice of beers (for take away or to be consumed on site, with some delicacies rotating on tap) and is certainly the place in Brussels where the most Italian beers are located.

De Biertempel

Rue du Marché Aux Herbes 56, 1000 Brussels

Located in the heart of the historic centre of Brussels, a stone's throw from the Grand Place. Since the closure of the historic Beer Temple, it has become the Beer Shop of reference for the many tourists who visit the city centre. Wide choice of beers (about 1000) and a chance to also buy souvenirs of the various breweries.

Bel-icious/D'en Belge

Rue de Flandre 88, 1000 Bruxelles

Small but well-stocked bottleshop run by the brother of the brewer of the Den Herberg brewery in Halle

The Beer House

Rue du Midi 28, 1000 Brussels

Another beer shop located in the city centre with about 250 beers for sale, including many great classics.

Les Caves de l'Ermitages

Rue Gheude 53, 1070 Anderlecht

Wed — Thu 13-19 Fri 13-20 Sat 11-18

This is a multifaceted project. In addition to being the beer shop of the Nano Brasserie de l'Ermitage, it is also their cellar for natural wines and storage room for mixed fermentation products. It offers a good selection of foreign beers, in particular from UK and Spain.

Les Fleurs du Malt

Av. du Roi Chevalier 45, 1200 Woluwe-Saint-Lambert
Tue — Sat 11.30-19

Located in the municipality of Woluwe-Saint Lambert, an arid place from the beer point of view. An excellent selection of Belgian craft beers is on offer. Tasting evenings and homebrewing classes are also organised.

Hop!

Av. des Celtes 22, 1040 Etterbeek
Mon — Sat 10.30-19.30

Gourmet shop with a good selection of beers, located a short distance from Merode metro, and the Cinquantaire Park.

Belgopop

Av. de Laeken 25, 1090 Jette
Wed — Sat 10-18 Sun 10-13

Concept store located in the municipality of Jette with all kinds of articles made in Belgium. It has a very good choice of beers, many from Brussels microbreweries.

Focus: Beer Mania

It would not have been possible for me not to interview the owner and founder of one of my favourite places in Brussels; Beer Mania. I developed a great part of my Belgian beer culture in this amazing place over long evenings tasting extraordinary beers with friends.

Over a long chat Michael told me of his incredible journey retracing the over 40 years of the existence of Beer Mania. A history intertwined with the history of beer in Brussels and around the world.

At the end of the chat, he gave me a present of a bottle containing the first batch of "Mea Culpa", the iconic beer he brews for Beer Mania.

Interview with Michael Efthekhari:

Michael, how and when did your adventure begin?

I opened the Beer Mania in 1981, it was the first Beer Shop in the world.

I've always been passionate about beer, I started drinking beer at the age of 9. Beer is more than a drink to me, it's a philosophy. In front of a beer, you can talk about everything; life, politics, love, problems. And you can talk about everything because you're drinking a beer. Wine is different, beer is more immediate, more sincere. Beer is culture, it is a tool that unites people. In my place I have seen people get to know each other, get married and come back with children.

And culture, unlike everything else, is not quantifiable and has immense value.

When I started my business beer was not a factor in Belgium.

In every corner of this country, people drank only local beers. In Flanders, there were no Wallonian beers, and there were no Flemish beers in Wallonia.

After the Second World War, the Belgian beer panorama was destroyed. Now it's starting to grow again.

When I started selling, beer was complicated. I started with 200 beers, then 300, then 400 and now I have almost 500. I almost have no room to keep them.

I was motivated by passion, but the first goal was to survive and pay the rent.

Belgian beer was not famous in the world, it has become so only in the last 20 years.

I travelled to the USA 25 years ago, no one knew what Belgium was, or where it was. Now, everyone knows Westvleteren, they know Belgian beers.

Today opening a bar is easy, opening a beer shop is easy. There are hundreds of them now. When I opened, people weren't used to drinking beer at home, they drank beer only at the bar. The idea of drinking a beer at home was inconceivable. A beer shop was useless, they said to me.

In Brussels, there were places where you got to with your car, you loaded a crate of water, one of lemonade and two of Jupiler and then you left by another exit.

In the supermarkets, there were only Jupiler, Stella, Virton (which no longer exists) and Guinness.

I have dedicated all my life, all my youth, all my energy to this project. And I have made my small contribution to make this drink famous.

Ten years after the opening of Beer Mania, I decided to open a bar also. Wine Bars were starting to open in Brussels. I opened a beer bar where you could buy beers and drink them too.

Unfortunately, some serious problems marked the beginning of my business; problems with the construction company led to my bar being closed for 7 years. I used my stock room as a store throughout that period. At the beginning, renovation works which should have lasted for only three months, took seven long years.

Luckily, I managed to keep the store open, otherwise I would have gone bankrupt. I spent 3 million Belgian francs, about EUR 8 000 on rent. I had to ask the bank continously for money.

I also spent a lot of money to rebuild the building where we are.

To diversify, I opened another beer shop in St. Gilles, Chaussee de Waterloo at 125. This was a project launched in partnership with a friend who retired for health reasons. I rented a place for three years. Unfortunately, I was not lucky with the staff I hired to help me.

The first had problems with alcohol, the second with drugs. Working in a beer shop exposes you to temptations. So, I sold the business despite having already paid 3 years of rent.

These two disasters have marked me both in my mood and in my bank account. I also wanted to open a brewery next to the beer shop but I did not have the resources to do so. I was exhausted because of these problems.

Then, working day and night, things got better and business also. In 1996, I created the world's first online shop, two months before Amazon's Jeff Bezos. Unfortunately, he was better at exploiting the idea than I was.

I had two employees taking care of the shipments. I became the second best customer of the FedEx shipping agency in Europe. Every day, we sent 15-20 boxes of beers to the USA.

Then came September 11 2001 which, in addition to changing the world, also changed the habits of American consumers. In the same period, Americans started importing beers and the market changed.

My orders from the US collapsed and I had to fire my employees.

My business reached its peak in the period prior to Covid. Covid dealt us a bad blow. Perhaps more than closures, what most harmed us was teleworking. Many of our regular customers have been teleworking, even from abroad.

In the last months of 2022, business improved to pre-covid levels.

If I have to summarise in a sentence, I would say; Love for beers and need to pay the rent.

Tell me more about your beer, Mea Culpa

As I told you, one of my goals was to open a brewery next to the beer shop. I had an agreement with the owner of the building close to the one we are now. I was young, I had money and energy. But then I had the problems I have just explained you.

So, I started brewing at another brewery. I had a friend who worked as a master brewer at the Van Steenberge brewery, the brewery that produces Gulden Draak. He had a small brewing equipment that he used to brew beer for himself and friends. I started there with him about 25 years ago.

I wanted a beer with special characteristics.

At the time, triples were fashionable. Before that it was the period of the pils, then blanche, then strong blond ale like Duvel, today is that of the IPA, and tomorrow of who knows what style.

I loved Orval, then I discovered the XX Bitter by De Ranke, which was a great revolution for my taste, I always drank it. I always saw my clients drink triple while I was drinking the XX Bitter.

Hence the idea of creating a recipe inspired by beers such as Westmalle Triple, Quintine Blonde, Orval and XX Bitte, my favourite beers.

I talked about the idea with my friend Kurt. We brewed 14 batches and after two years of work we found the right recipe.

I originally called it Carpe Diem. But then I received a letter from a lawyer in the Netherlands. They asked me for damages of EUR 2 000 because the brand belonged to Heineken and I was causing them damage.

I was devastated, after all the time I had devoted to the project. Unfortunately, I had only registered the trademark in Belgium while I should have made a registration for the Benelux or perhaps for the whole European Community.

I talked to my lawyer and she found a solution; since I had not yet sold a bottle, we wrote to them that it was a simple mistake and that we would not sell that beer. Thankfully, they accepted and did not ask me for anything.

I was safe but I still had a beer to sell, with no name left.

At the time, I had 7-8 customers who were here every day. It was a heterogeneous group with different geographical origins. I asked them to do a "beer storming" and help me find a name for my creation.

One of these, an old English gentleman, who was a teacher at the European School, one evening, when he was a little bit drunk, proposed as a name "Mea Culpa". I loved it and adopted it.

For about 7 years, I have been producing it at De Ranke, we use the same hops as the XX Bitter and is composed of ten different ingredients.

The Mea Culpa has always been a small production. I don't export it even though a lot of people have asked for it. I only send it to a trusted customer in Japan.

What type of customers do you have?

I am the official supplier of the American Embassy in Brussels. I met and served beer to people such as Bush, Biden, Blair, Chirac, Schroder, the Deep Purple music band and many Belgian politicians.

Every person in Brussels knows Beer Mania, we have always been a reference point. Before the coming of big mass bars like Delirium, people came here. We are on the tourist guides together with attractions such as the Atomium or the Manneken Pis.

Today, we have many Italian and Spanish customers; and then a little bit of everything. We lost many American customers after September 11 and the various waves of terror attacks in Europe. I have the impression that Americans are travelling less in Europe than before. And Brexit cleared Brussels of British people, who were my great clients.

How do you think the Brussels beer scene will evolve in the coming years?

There is a lot of turmoil but I think that most of the breweries or beer firms that produce only IPAs and similar ones will not last long. These are random productions that will not last long because the fashion for this beer style will not last long.

Brussels is saturated. The bars all open in the same areas. You can't have any more. Many have lost customers even though they are open for the entire day.

They all have the same beers, they offer nothing new.

Some old bars with tradition will survive.

Today, people like canned beer. I don't like beer in cans. It's not in the Belgian beer culture, it's an American model that young people like. But I have to sell them because people ask me for them and clearly I can't let my customers go to my competitors.

What's about the future of Beer Mania?

We are happy. We're two and we'll stay two, my wife and me. We work hard but I don't want to change my business model.

People come here for Beer Mania. We are not in a touristic place; those who come here come here for us. I have loyal customers. No one comes at random, we are in a neighbourhood with few attractions.

People come for the concept that characterises Beer Mania; a comfortable place, good choice of beers, served at the right temperature, in the correct and clean glasses. And they come here for me and for my wife. We are this and we do not want to change it.

Restaurants

One of the most interesting features, and less known to the general public, of beer is the great potential to pair it with food. Thanks to the wide spectrum of aromas and flavours, it is easy to find the right beer for any dish, much easier than with wine.

Beer is in fact a very versatile drink with infinite aroma and taste connotations. Every characteristic linked to taste (acid, bitter, sweet, jump... even umami), aromas, body and alcohol can be traced in the immense beer landscape.

Moreover, the immense Belgian beer landscape offers many possibilities. Beer and food are therefore a winning partnership. Belgian cuisine, while not offering the richness and variety of the Mediterranean cuisine presents several interesting dishes.

In this chapter, you will find the best restaurants in Brussels taking in to account the food and the menu of beers.

Nuetnigenough

Rue du Lombard 25, Brussels 1000 - www.nuetnigenough.be

This Brussels brasserie welcomes "Nuetnigenough's" (who has never had enough) and gourmands offering a menu with about fifty beers, which includes some pearls of Belgian breweries dedicated to traditional production. The menu boasts great classics at 'Nuetnigenough' that complete a series of old-fashioned recipes.

Ploegamans

Rue Haute 148, 1000 Brussels

Classic old-style brasserie typical of the Marolles area. Every detail, from the decor to the menu is typical of the classic Belgian cuisine.

In't Spinnekopke

Place du Jardin aux fleurs 1, Brussels 1000 - www.spinnekopke.be

Opened in a building used since 1792 as a post station for post chaises Here you can taste all Belgian specialties and other beer related recipes. In 2024, they launched their own geuze in collaboration with Den Herberg.

Les Brigittines

Place de la Chapelle 5, Brussels 1000 - www.lesbrigittines.com

Les Brigitinnes Restaurant is located in the heart of Brussels, a stone's throw from the Grand Place, the Palais de Justice and the Sablon and Marolles districts. In the particular atmosphere of its Liberty-style rooms, it offers classic French-Belgian cuisine, based on fresh seasonal products and beer.

Bier Circus

Rue de l'Enseignement 57, Brussels 1000 - www.bier-circus.be

Traditional beer-based cuisine, a sacred place for true beer lovers.

Belga Queen

Rue Fossé aux loups 32, Brussels 1000 - www.belgaqueen.be

This majestic 18th century building, which once housed a hotel and a bank, was pleasantly converted and turned into a restaurant. The varied menu is accompanied by a long list of Belgian beers.

Cheese&Beer

Rue des Bouchers 30, 1000 Bruxelles
https://lescheeseandbeer.com/

"Pop up "restaurant specialised in pairing cheese and beer.

Bia Mara

Rue du Marché aux Poulets 41, 1000 Brussels

Pl. de Londres 1, 1050 Ixelles - https://www.biamara.com/

Bia Mara in Gaelic means "seafood". Fresh and quality seafood is at the heart of what, starting from a street food kiosk in Dublin, has become a chain of successful restaurants in Belgium. More than 40 different recipes from Fish&Chips and an interesting beer card with several beer from Brasserie de la Senne.

Le Clan des Belges

Rue de la Paix 20, 1050 Ixelles - https://www.leclandesbelges.com/

A restaurant located in the heart of Ixelles, in front of the Church of Saint Boniface. Atmosphere of the 20s, classic

Belgian cuisine and excellent choice of beers. For quality-price ratio, it is probably one of the best in the city.

Les Brassins

Rue Keyenveld 36, 1050 Ixelles - http://www.lesbrassins.be/

Classic Belgian Brasserie, a stone's throw from the colourful African district of Matongè. It offers excellent Belgian classics and a great choice of beers.

Liesse

Avenue Adolphe Demeur 57, 1060 St. Gilles - http://www.liessebxl.be

French restaurant much loved by beer geeks for its excellent choice of craft beers and its rich variety of Cantillon.

Le âne verte

Rue Royale-Sainte-Marie 11, 1030 Schaerbeek - https://www.anevert.be

Family restaurant of traditional Belgian cuisine located in the heart of Schaerbeek with a good mane of beers and lambic.

L'Horloge du Sud

Rue du Trône 141, 1050 Ixelles - https://horlogedusud.be

This corner restaurant, located between the European Quarter and the Matongé district, offers a wonderful blend of African cuisine and a great choice of Belgian beers.

Brasserie Le Miroir

PL. Reine Astrid 24/26, 1090 Jette - https://brasserielemiroirjette.be/

If you happen to be in the municipality of Jette, Brasserie Le Miroir is definitely the best place to eat. Classic Belgian cuisine and good choice of beers. For Pils lovers, the Crystal (of Alken Maes) is served directly from the tank.

Au Stekerlapatte

Rue des Prêtres 4, 1000 Brussels - https://www.austekerlapatte.be/en/

Excellent Belgian restaurant with French influences located behind the imposing building of the Courthouse. Good choice of beers and lambic.

La Villette

Rue du Vieux Marché aux Grains 3, 1000 Brussels - http://www.la-villette.be

Restaurant located in an old Brussels estaminet. Typical Belgian cuisine and excellent choice of beers including Cantillon on tap.

Pistolet Original

Rue Joseph Stevens 26, 1000 Bruxelles - https://www.pistolet-original.be/

Counter where people enjoy delicious "pistolets," distinctive home-made stuffed rolls garnished with "Americain préparé" meat or with grey shrimps or any number of other local products.

Au Repos De la Montagne

Montagne de Saint-Job 39, 1180 Uccle
Tue – Sat 17-23 Sun – Mon closed

Historic Estaminet located in a bucolic street in the heart of the Saint-Job district in Uccle. Old-world ambience, almost exclusively local clientele and a good selection of craft beers and natural wines.

Les Petits Bouchons

Chaussée d'Alsemberg 832, Uccle
Tue – Sat 17-23 Sun – Mon closed

Classic Belgian bistro with good food and a good selection of craft beers. It reminds to 'Les Brigittines' where the owner, Tom, worked in the past.

Restaurant Briefing

Chau. de Tervueren 137, 1160 Auderghem
https://le-briefing.be/

A classic Belgian restaurant with a good beer choice. Here you can find the "local" beers from Bieres Artisanales Waterghem.

MangiaSempre

Rue des Alliés 196, 1190 Forest
Tue – Fri 10-19 Sat 10-18 Sun – Mon closed.

Mangia Sempre, a perfect place for an Italian aperitivo. Giulia, the Italian owner from Perugia, has created this sweet little shop. It has not only great cheeses and meats to sample on their terrace but it's also a store with delicious pasta, sauces and other Italian products to cook at home. You can wash that all down with natural wines or beers from Brasserie Cantillon and other local breweries.

Focus: Restobières

The Restobières restaurant, located on Rue des Renards 9, was definitely one of the most popular beer restaurants in the world.

Unfortunately, in May 2021, it was closed and bankrupt due to the reduced turnover of the COVID 19 pandemic. Opened in 1987 by talented chef Alain Fayt, Restobières was able to combine typical Belgian cuisine with a splendid selection of craft beers, also used as a base for recipes. Among the most popular dishes were the carbonade flamande at Rodenbach Grand Cru, the Gueuze rabbit at Girardin, the calf blanquette at Dulle Teve by De Dolle and the mussels at Hommelbier. The Restobières was also known for its endless collection of memorabilia and ancient kitchen items (bottles, dishes for asparagus, coffee grinder, etc.). In recent years, moreover, Alain Fayt had set up a tasting room furnished with vintage games, in the back shop

The good news is that it should reopen in the coming months. The owner of the historic art-déco Verschueren brasserie, Robert Van Craen, has announced the purchase of the famous restaurant Restobières which will reopen after the necessary renovations.

Beer festivals and events in Brussels

Brassin Public Cantillon

This is the most anticipated appointment for Lambic lovers. Taking place twice a year within the Brasserie Cantillon, usually on the second Saturday of November and the first Saturday of March, those dates mark the beginning and end of Lambic production. In recent years, due to climate change and the consequent increase in temperatures even at these latitudes, the date has often been delayed. During the "Brassin" there are tours in English, French, Dutch and Italian.

Quintessence Brassicole Cantillon

An event as spectacular as it is difficult to access (due to the difficulty in finding tickets given the speed at which they are sold online). It is held every two years in May and consists of a tour inside the Brasserie Cantillon with a dozen stops in various locations to taste different products combined with cheeses, cold cuts and desserts produced by local artisans. In recent editions, it has been organised in cooperation with the American breweries Russian River and Allagash Brewing Company. The next edition will involve some breweries based in Brussels.

Given the great demand, and the high number of tourists from all over the world who arrive, there are now numerous parallel events where you can taste some of the beers present at Quintessence and other Cantillon products. Recently, parallel events were organised by the Brasserie de l'Ermitage, the Moeder Lambic, La Tana and restaurants such as Les Brigittines, Pasta Madre (closed at the end of 2022) and Nuetnigenough.

Zwanze Day

In the Brussels dialect, the word "Zwanze" refers to a sense of humour of sarcastic style. Zwanze Day is held every year on the last Saturday of September. Cantillon's successful Zwanze event series began in 2008 when a special Lambic was put on sale with the addition of rhubarb. Since then, it has become a real celebration, held in venues all along Europe, and around the world. Usually, the Zwanze is released simultaneously in all the hosted locations.

Belgian Beer Week End

The Belgian Beer Weekend, organised by the Belgian Brewers Federation, is one of the most famous events in the Belgian beer scene. It is held during the first weekend of September in the beautiful setting of the Grand Place.

Within a few hundred metres, among the stands set up on the Grand Place, the most important breweries of the country are gathered in a goliardic atmosphere, making it a very popular event for tourists and beer enthusiasts.

In addition to tasting the beers, you can watch the traditional historical parade of brewers, the parade of ancient chariots, and the blessing of the beer barrel that is offered to Sant'Arnold, patron of the brewers.

Over the two days, at the Hotel de Ville, the Brussels City Hall, located on the Grand Place, the ceremony of the appointment of the new members of the Chevalerie du Fourquet des Brasseurs, takes place. The Fourquet is the name of the tool, similar to the pitchfork, which in ancient times was used by the master brewer.

Wanderlust

Organised by the Brussels Beer Project every year in September. Initially it was held in the Tours&Taxis area, along the Brussels Canal. In recent years it has been organised at Place Vismet, in the beautiful setting of Saint Catherine. In addition to the Brussels Beer Project beers, you can taste beer from breweries from all over the world.

SWAFFs

Another festival with a strong "Craft" and "beer geek" imprint. Co-organised by the Dynamo and Barboteur bars, it takes place every year in May. The breweries present are an interesting mix between Brussels and foreign entities. It is possible to work as a volunteer at this festival. The most recent event took place at the creative centre LaVallée in Molenbeek.

BXL Beer Fest

Co-organised by the owners of the Moeder Lambic and Nuetnigenough, it takes place every year at the end of August on the Tours&Taxis site. This festival came into being with the stated goal of becoming the Festival of Craft Beer par excellence in Brussels. The focus is on the craft breweries, strictly independent, with a good mix between Belgian and Brussels entities and international guests.

Over the weekend, workshops and tastings are also organised.

It is also possible to work there as a volunteer.

Beer Bazaar

Held between the end of September and the beginning of October on the site of See U Brussels (a former military barracks where housing for university and non-university people will be built, but which in the meantime hosts cultural events and activities). Microbreweries and Brussels beer firms are usually involved.

Festival de la Bière Woluwe-Saint-Pierre

Organised every year in September by the Brussels Commune of Woluwe Saint-Pierre on the Place des Maïeurs. There is a mix of Brussels and Belgian breweries.

Museums

Brussels is a city with many museums and being the Beer Capital, you should not miss those dedicated to our favourite drink.

Belgian Brewers Museum

Grand-Place 10, 1000 Brussels
Wed — Sat 11-18

Located in the Maison des Brasseurs on the Grand Place, the headquarters of the Association of Beer Producers in Belgium. The exhibition is located in the basement where in a re-construction of a medieval tavern, with barrels and wooden boards, ancient brewing equipment is on display. In another room, there is more modern equipment. A video shows the entire production process. The tour ends with one tasting in the well-stocked museum cafe. The entrance fee is EUR 5.

Musée Schaerbeekois de la bière

Louis Bertrandlaan 33/35, 1030 Schaarbeek
Wed and Sat 14-18

The museum was launched in 1993 by eleven beer enthusiasts. The municipality of Schaerbeek made an unused section of a school in rue de la Ruche available to them.

One of the founding members made his collection of over 300 Belgian beers available as the starting point for the museum. From there the collection of objects related to the world of beer among various breweries and brocante (markets) began.

The museum was inaugurated on 26 March 1994 and at that time had two rooms and a small estaminet. Two years later, in 1996, a new room with a larger estaminet was added.

Today the museum dislays a collection of more than 2500 bottles of Belgian beers and 5000 glasses. There is also old equipment for brewing beer, utensils, signs and advertising items and documents about old breweries.

The entrance fee is EUR 5 and entitles you to a tasting of 12.5 cl of a "Schaerbeekoise" (Brune of 9 % brassed by the Van Den Bossche brewery exclusively for the museum) or an "Eizelskop" (Triple of 8 degrees produced by Brussels Brasserie de l'Ermitage exclusively for the museum). Both the beers can be purchased at the shop.

Musée bruxellois de la gueuze

See Cantillon page 16.

Belgian Beer World

The year 2023 saw the opening of the Belgian Beer World, in the Bourse building. More than a museum, it is a large, dynamic and interactive visitor centre dedicated to Belgian beer modelled on the Guinness Storehouse in Dublin and the Heineken Experience in Amsterdam. Visitors have the chance to discover the culture of beer in Belgium at their own pace and according to their tastes and interests.

The tour last about an hour and a half and includes a historical part and a part dedicated to ingredients and brewing.

The Bourse building is a very eclectic neo-classical building built between 1868 and 1873 by architect Leon-Pierre Susy. The sculptures were created by several artists including Auguste Rodin. The building was built on a site that housed the tomb of the legendary Duke of Brabant Jan Primus I, better known as Gambrinus.

Renovations started in 2020, but since the building is a UNESCO monument, the works took longer than usual. The Belgian Beer World is set to become a major tourist attraction with 400,000 visitors expected per year. This is a project very much sought by the sector, so much that over a hundred Belgian breweries have invested more than 5 million euros in the project.

To understand more about the project I interviewed Sven Gatz, Minister of Culture of the Brussels-Capital Region, and also a great expert and beer enthusiast.

Sven Gazt is the brains and driving force behind this project. Without his foresight and tenacity, the Belgian Beer World project would not have seen light.

Sven Gatz is also the author of several books on beer including one of the guides from which I took inspiration for this book. Taking advantage of his generosity and availability I also took the opportunity to ask him about his vision of the future of beer in Brussels.

Interview with Minister of Culture of the Brussels-Capital Region, Sven Gazt:

Minister Gazt, how did the idea of the Belgian Beer World arise?

In 2006 I was on holiday in Dublin with my wife. We visited the Guinness Storehouse and I was positively impressed. It is a major investment aimed at promoting beer culture to the general public, although in that case a single brand.

I then visited Heineken Experience in Amsterdam, the Scotch Whisky Experience in Edinburgh and the Citè du Vin in Bordeaux.

I am a great fan of beer, and I have always considered it important to let Belgians and those who visit this country know this extraordinary drink. At the time, I was a Member of the Parliament and I started to think about how to develop something like this in Brussels.

I convened a press conference at the old Belle-Vue at Kanaal, in the building that today houses the MIMA Museum. I wanted to establish the museum there, but AB Inbev had other plans. The media welcomed the idea well and so I decided to continue talking to colleagues, launching a feasibility study and evaluating various locations.

In 2011, after 16 years in Parliament, I decided to change my life and I left politics. At the suggestion of Michel Moortgaat, whom I had known for some time having studied together, I became Director of the Belgian Brewers.

Also in 2011 Philippe Close, today Mayor of Brussels, and then Councillor for Tourism, to whom I had talked to about the project, called me. He told me that the city of Brussels had bought the Bourse building and proposed that location for my project.

So I asked the brewers to take part in it and so it all started.

Projects of this kind are developed by building parallel alliances.

In the meantime, in 2014, I was called to be Minister of Culture. This was the dream of my life, and allowed me to continue working on the project from an institutional position.

In 2015, the city officially presented the Belgian Beer World project in the Bourse building. The legal company we set up is by two-thirds controlled by the City of Brussels and the remaining third by brewers, each of them having invested a share.

The project would not have been feasible without the involvement of the two biggest industrial players in the Belgian beer world; AB Inbev and Duvel Moortgat. But it would not have been credible without the presence of other independent breweries as well. This is why we created a quota system that would allow even smaller breweries, with fewer resources, to participate in the project. As of today, we have involved 106 breweries from all over Belgium and also some breweries from Brussels since the Brussels beer scene could not be left out. We also have the Trappists, who also convinced Westlvleteren to participate in the project. It will be a roof for everyone.

The renovation of the building is almost complete and we aim for the official opening in 2023.

With the Belgian Beer World, we want to take Belgian beer culture to another cultural level. Beer has always been a combination of culture and economy. We want a place where tourists want to go, like the Guinness Storehouse, which is also visited by people who don't necessarily like beer.

How will it works in practice?

70% will be for experience and 30% a museum. The building will be open all day. The large central hall will be transformed into a public space that will host events and exhibitions. There will be various entrances, one will be on the side towards the Grand Place, others in the side streets to the Bourse.

Belgian Beer World will occupy the first and second floor. It will culminate with a rooftop bar where you can taste one or two beers included in the entrance ticket. It provides a mix of history and sensory experiences.

Below the Bourse, a 13rd century tomb of the Duke of Brabant John I, also known as Jan Primus or Gambrinus, the king of beer, was discovered. The tomb site will be accessible.

The hope is that the Belgian Beer World will be one of the biggest tourist attractions in Brussels.

How do you think the Brussels beer scene will evolve in the coming years?

I think there are good prospects. More and more, people like products made locally and with local ingredients.

People are willing to pay more to drink better, and drink local products.

First in Belgium we had the obsession that beer should be as cheap as possible. Now people are not afraid to have to pay 50 cents or even EUR 1 more.

Fifteen years ago, nobody imagined that Belgium would have 400 active breweries.

Five years ago, it was said that the market was saturated. It wasn't. There has been progressive development.

In Brussels, for reasons of cost, many breweries open up in less attractive areas and their presence helps to change these neighbourhoods. It's a sort of "beer gentrification". Twenty years ago we all thought that the beer industry had conquered Brussels, now the "smalls" are coming back. The city needs both actors. Signifying this are the two great brewing festivals that our city hosts; the Belgian Beer Weekend at the Grand Place, and the BXL Beer Fest, two different events but with full participation.

What is your favourite beer from a Brussels brewery?

In general, I love the styles that are carried on traditionally. They are the emblem of our brewing culture.

Of the several beers I like, I would like to mention three; Gueuze of Cantillon because the revival of the Gueuze was a revival for me too. Zinnebir that changed the history of beer in the city. And then the Pico Nova, the beer without alcohol of the Brussels Beer Project, the best of its kind.

Beer Spa

For an all-round total beer experience, you should not miss a beer spa. A concept already widespread in European countries such as Germany and the Czech Republic, it made its appearance in Brussels in 2021 when, almost simultaneously, two Beer Spas opened.

The Beer Spa Experience

Rue Scailquin 43/00, 1210 Saint-Josse-ten-Noode
Mon — Thu 17.30-21 Fri — Sun 12.30-21

For 45 minutes, you can be immersed into, and taste, the Baptist, a blonde of the Van Steenberge brewery.

Bath&Barley — The Belgian Beer Spa

Rue de l'Ecuyer 34, 1000 Brussels
Wed 16.30-22 Thu 15-22 Fri 13.30-22 Sat 11-22 Sun 12-21

At Bath&Barley, you will immerse yourself in a bath with the ingredients of beer; water (hot), hop, barley and yeast. You can choose from the hops selected by the Brussels Beer Project, Oud Berseel and Palm breweries and taste an Estaminet, the Pils of the Palm brewery, or a "beer flight" of three beers from the three breweries already mentioned combined with three chocolates from the Maitre Chocolatier Frédéric Blondeel.

Belgian Beer Styles

"Beer doesn't exist, there are beers". This famous sentence by Kuaska, one of the best Italian beer connoisseur, summarises in a simple but effective way the concept behind our favourite drink.

Beer is a product characterised by a considerable variety of types, technically called "style". The "style" is the "passport" of beer; it defines a priori parameters such as history, production method, ingredients, colour, aroma, flavour and alcohol content.

Beer style theory is largely based on Fred Eckhardt's work "The Essentials of Beer Style", published in 1989, which was adopted by the Beer Judge Certification Program (BJCP) for the International Classification of Beer Styles.

In general, beers can be divided into three large macro categories compared to the type of fermentation;

Ale: derived from "high fermentation", thanks to Saccharomyces cerevisiae, a top fermenting yeast, which carries out the process at a temperature between 16 and 23 °C.

Lager: produced by the process of "low fermentation", conducted by the Saccharomyces carlsbergensis, a bottom fermenting yeast. The vast majority of the beers produced in the world are Lagers.

Lambic: wild/spontaneous fermentation, beers fermented with bacteria or non-Saccharomyces yeast.

Within these "macro-styles", there is a multitude of technical facets.

Knowing the styles that characterises the range of beer is a form of knowledge that enriches you and makes you a more aware and discerning consumer.

Belgium is a country with a most important beer tradition. Below, you will find an overview of the "Belgium" beer styles.

Saison

The Saisons were once produced towards the end of winter to be consumed in the warmer months by the seasonal workers employed in the fields, the so-called "saisonnières". The province of Hainaut in the Walloon region was, and still is, the reference area for this style of beer.

These beers had to have the ability to preserve themselves for a long time without being too alcoholic (since there were consumed during the work on the fields). For this reason, they were produced with mixtures of "Gruyt" spices and/or hops that could vary in composition depending on the territory. Very often they tasted acidic.

The decisive factor in determining the profile of a Saison has always been that of fermentation. Traditionally, it relied on mixed crops of yeasts, wild and otherwise, often contaminated with lactobacilli, and able to attenuate the wort in a decidedly energetic way (spontaneous procedures were not to be excluded completely).

Today, Saisons are available all year round, and the style has become one of the most replicated and interpreted styles worldwide. The colour ranges from golden to brown; the gradation from 3.5 % to 9.5 %.

They are usually easy to drink beers characterised by aromatic compounds, floral sensations, fruity, spicy and often acidulous.

The best example is the Saison Dupont.

Blanche\Wit

Literally, "White Beer". Historic Belgian style originally from the city of Hoegaarden in the Flemish Brabant. This style practically disappeared in the 1950s. It was kept alive by Pierre Celis, a dairyman who with his brewery (De Kuis, which later became Hoegaarden, and since 1988 is owned by the giant AB InBev) made the style famous.

They are light-coloured beers, straw or parchment yellow, or citrus and spicy aroma, refreshing and pleasantly acidic. They are produced with a mixture of barley malt and non-malted wheat. The use of hops is limited and as spices there are curacao and coriander. They are very light beers with a gradient of between 4.5 and 5.5 degrees.

An excellent example is the Blanche de Namur of Brasserie du Bocq.

Blonde

The Blond (or Blonde Ale) is the Belgian answer to the advent of German lagers.

These are high fermentation beers, the strains used are of the species Saccharomyces cerevisiae and contribute to the definition of the aromatic profile thanks to the production of esters and phenols.

The fermentable base consists largely of pils malt, usually supplemented by aromatic malts. Hops often belong to classic European varieties, such as Saaz, Styrian Glondings and East Kent Goldings, and are only rarely of Belgian origin.

In some cases, blonde ale also includes the addition of spices (coriander, citrus peel, ginger, etc.), but their aromatic intake must remain in the background and not cover the organoleptic characteristics coming from the other ingredients. Often, the spicy notes we find inside these beers are derived from yeast and not from other elements. Belgium's Blond Ale starts from 6 % to reach 7.5 %. Nevertheless, they can skilfully hide their not indifferent alcohol content.

A good example of Blonde Ale is Brouwerij Kerkom's Bink.

Dubbel

The origins of this style are difficult to date but should probably be dated to the beginning of monastic brewing.

The Dubbel are characterised by a persistent, abundant and cappuccino foam and are amber/dark colour. They are beers with an aroma characterised by spices and red fruits and a moderately caramelised taste with mild ethyl notes. Dubbels are usually between 6.5 and 7 %.

A great example is the Westmalle Dubbel Trappist beer.

Tripel

The definition of Tripel beer began to appear in the early 1930s to indicate strong golden beers and distinguish them from strong beers that were generally referred to as "Dubbel".

The famous "Beer Hunter" Michael Jackson traces the intuition to Hendrik Verlinden, who at the time collaborated with the monks of Westmalle.

Generally, these are beers with dense, white, creamy and persistent foam, with a golden colour. The scentnose offers a composite range of aromas ranging from yellow fruit to spices. The taste tends to bitter with a dry finish enriched by spicy-fruity notes given by yeast.

Feeling on the palate; body from medium-light to medium, significant gassing. The alcohol level is well hidden and is felt with a slight warming sensation of the oral cavity. They are surprisingly, and dangerously, drinkable despite their average gradation ranges from 7.5 % to 9.5 %.

An excellent example of Triple is the Trappist Westmalle Tripel.

Belgian Strong Golden Ale

They are among the most popular Belgian beer styles. These are high-alcohol beers (above 7 %) structured mainly, in a sensory way, around the work of the yeasts (so of their fruity-spice esters) and marked by an alcoholic vigour only partially masked by counterweight elements, such as the dryness of the mouth and the bitter content brought by the hops.

They appeared after the First World War on the basis of the needs highlighted by an audience of consumers rather oriented towards the golden beers.

The malt used is mostly Pils, with possible use of sugar (10-20 % maximum) to increase the alcohol content without weighing on the final density. Hop is not the element in the spotlight for this style, but it plays an important role in balance. The main characterisation occurs thanks to the work of yeast.

In the glass, we find a beer of straw colour to golden; the aromas balanced between floral currents from hops, fruity (pear, apple, apricot) and spicy (phenols) from fermenting inputs. Energetic taste, in line with the smell, with a bitter tone between medium and high. They have an important alcohol content, between 8 and 10 degrees, but the best interpretations are dangerously drinkable.

One of the best example of Belgian Strong Golden Ale is the Duvel, the flag beer of Duvel Moortgat.

Belgian Strong Dark Ale

According to the BJCP guidelines, they are the equivalent of Quadrupel. Belgian Strong Dark Ales are beers with a colour ranging from intense amber to brown with an alcohol content ranging from 8 to 12 %. The aromas range from toasted caramel, to dark honey, to dried fruit with notes of spices such as vanilla and liquorice. The taste is warm, fortified and with a bitter tone.

In this category, we find famous beers such as Rochefort 10, Chimay Blue and the legendary Westvleteren 12.

Special Belge

Also known as Belgian Pale Ale.

It is a little known and little replicated style. They were developed as the Belgian response to the English Pale

Ales from which they take the use of some varieties of hops and some strains of yeast.

Today, the Speciale Belge have a colour that varies between the amber and the brown and are low alcoholic (between 4.8 and 5.5 % by volume). They are characterised by an aroma and a taste of toasted malt and an aftertaste that brings back caramel, hazelnut and honey flavours.

Lambic and Gueuze

Lambic are spontaneously fermented beers from Pajotteland (also part of the Brussels area corresponding to the municipality of Anderlecht).

Lambic is produced with a mixture of barley malt and non-malted wheat, usually in a 60/40 ratio (a 1965 law requires a minimum percentage of wheat of 30 %); the hops used shall have at least two years of preservation, in order to eliminate all the aromatic components and minimise the bitter component. The wort is left in contact with the air, fermentation takes place thanks to mixtures of wild yeasts and microorganisms present in the environment of this area.

There is also the aging process in barrels; after a night of cooling in the open tub, the wort is poured into wooden barrels where it will ferment and will remain ripe for at least one year. In this period of time, the beer gradually reduces its natural carbonation (by virtue of the permeability of the wood) and ferments thanks to a mix of particular yeasts, the most important of which are the brettanomicetes that give it those unmistakable and complex fruity and "cellar" notes, that dry, tannic sometimes astringent taste.

The olfactory sensations are those reminiscent of flowers, fresh citrus fruits and yogurt. The taste is acidic and astringent. The alcohol content is medium-low. It should be noted that Lambic is produced only in the cold months (from autumn to spring).

It is a unique product, defined by one of its most famous producers, Frank Boon, "the missing link between wine and beer" and by the brewer and writer Jef Van den Steen "the oldest style of modern beers".

Lambic can stay in barrel for more than a year, this is the premise for the creation of Gueuze, which are nothing more than Lambic blends of different ages in which the youngest, still quite rich in fermentable sugars, brings the right carbonation. The Geuze are characterised by greater sparkiness. The gradation ranges from 5 to 8 %.

There are also the Faro (a style that is difficult to find) that are obtained by mixing Lambic and candied sugar, the Kriek (Lambic with the addition of cherries) and Framboise (Lambic with the addition of raspberries). Recently the Druiven lambic (Lambic with grapes) have come to prominence.

The examples par excellence of these categories are the Lambic and the Gueuze of Cantillon.

Abbey Beers vs Trappist Beers

Very often the terms "abbey" and "Trappist" are used almost as synonyms, in a decidedly improper way.

Abbey Beers

The term abbey beers means a rather wide range of beers styles. It originally indicated beverages produced in Belgian and Dutch monasteries.

Today, the link with the abbeys has often ceased (except for some beers such as Val-Dieu and Abbaye d'Aulnee) beers are brewed in commercial breweries that have the authorisation to operate under the license of a still active abbey or using the name of a disused monastery.

These breweries exploit the brand but use the original recipes, keeping the tradition alive.

Trappist Beers

The term "Trappist" beer does not indicate a precise style and can only be defined as such if it follows a set of well-defined rules. The requirements to use this title and the well-known red hexagonal logo "Authentic Trappist Product" are as follows:

- Beer must be brewed inside a monastery;
- The production process must take place under the control of the monastic community;
- Sales revenues must be used for charitable purposes.

In Belgium, there are still five Trappist monasteries producing beer; Westmalle, Westvleteren, Chimay, Orval and Rochefort. A sixth, Achel, lost the Trappist mark in 2021 because the local community of monks in the monastery of Saint Benedict of Hamont-Achel is no longer active. To be precise, beer production still takes place inside the abbey, but there no longer is a monk who can at least supervise it. Therefore, one of the three criteria necessary to define a Trappist brewery had ceased to exist.

Lost Beer Styles of Belgium

For those who want to deepen their knowledge about the styles of Belgian beer, the best book is the "Traite complet de la fabrication des bieres et de la distillation des grains" by G. Lacambre, a French scientist living in Belgium who worked as a consultant for the Brasserie La Vignette, bringing numerous innovations. In the work, published in 1851, he described many Flemish and Walloon styles that have now disappeared or turned into "modern" brands.

About these "lost styles" speaks also the American beer guru Randy Moscher.

Barley Beers from Antwerp

In the past, Antwerp was famous for the Bière d'Orge d'Anvers (Barley Beer of Antwerp), produced in their best versions with only barley malt (alternatively they provided a small percentage of wheat or oats). They were not very alcoholic beers (5 % — 6 %), discreetly hoppy with aroma varieties and aged at least six months, although older batches were also used, blended with young or sweetened versions, with the addition of caramel syrup. Their colour was between amber and brown, but sometimes chalk was added to the boiler to darken the wort.

Uytzet or Flanders Barley Beer

Typical of the Ghent area, they were produced with amber malts and small percentages of wheat and/or oats. They had moderate hops and existed in two versions based on their alcohol content; ordinary (3.2 %) or double (4.5 %).

In addition, they were brewed in a relatively short time thanks to vigorous fermentation and very quick boiling, following a rather curious (and cumbersome) productive process- the wort cooled after boiling was divided into small containers, where the yeast was inoculated; later some of the liquid in fermentation was removed and added new unfermented must.

Brown Beers from Flanders

The ancestor of what is now called Flemish Red Ale (Western Flanders) and Oud Bruin (Eastern Flanders). The boiling was very long and could take up to 20 hours.

Maastricht Beers

A type of dark beer produced in Flanders, but mainly found in the inner territories of the Netherlands. Their name was associated with other Dutch cities such as Boscoducale and Masek. The recipe for the style provided that the grist was composed of durum wheat, malted spelt and wheat with low protein content, with a very low hop.

Barley beers from Wallonia

This definition included very different productions in colour and organoleptic characteristics, although the alcohol content was always around 4 % — 5 %. Despite the name, the barley beers typical of Liège and Mons contained percentages of durum wheat with high protein content, spelt, oats and even (in some cases) buckwheat and beans. They were aged for 4-6 months.

Diest

Diest is a municipality in Flemish Brabant, known in the past for this beer specialty, produced with barley malt, non-malted wheat and oats. The Diest were quite nutritious beers. They existed in two variants, which, among other things, differed in percentages of cereals used. The Gulde Bier or Bière de cabaret (milk 44 %, wheat 40 %, oats 16 %) were viscous and slightly sweet; the real Diest (malt 55 %, wheat 30 %, oats 15 %) were in turn available in two versions, light and "double".

Brown beers from Mechelen

They were very dark beers due to a very long boiling period, which could last as long as 10-12 hours and provide for the addition of chalk to darken the wort. They were made by combining a third (or a quarter) of aged beer with a remaining part of young beer and achieving a very similar result to Oud Bruin and Flemish Red Ale.

Beers of Hoegaarden

These are the ancestors of the Blanche (or Witbier). They were composed of barley malt (63 %), wheat not malted (21 %) and oats (16 %). They were soft and thirst-quenching beers and characterised by a certain acidity.

Peetermann and Cavesse

The Peetermann, one of the variants of Hoegaarden wheat beers, were typical of Leuven, and intensely amber due to the addition of chalk during mapping. They were little attenuated and described as "viscous", probably due to their opalescence.

Cavesse

The Cavesse, typical of Lier, used the same ingredients as Hoegaarden beers, but with slightly different percentages: thus barley malt (67 %), wheat (13 %) and oats (20 %).

Beers of Liège

They were also known as Saison of Liège but had nothing to do with the classic Saison. They were made with barley malt, malted spelt, oats and wheat. They were available in two versions: Bière jeune, i.e. "young beer", and Bière de saison, i.e. "season beer". In the second case they were stronger and the "season" they referred to was winter, when most consumption occurred. The bière de saisons were drunk after a minimum of three or four months of maturation and sometimes their preservation lasted for up to one or two years. In this case, it is easy to imagine that an intrusion of wild yeasts developed, which made the beer more attenuated and with vinous and funky notes.

Belgian cuisine

Belgium, due to its proximity to France, has a well-established and rather interesting gastronomic tradition. Obviously, you have come to Belgium for beers, but in this section you will find some tips to eat something good and typical.

Frites/Frieten

The famous "Frites" (fried potato chips) are a real specialty of the country.

Frites in Belgium are considered street food and are served from kiosks. Usually, it is possible to combine them with sauces of various types (I recommend Andalouse, Poivre and Pili Pili).

In Brussels, the best places to eat Frites are the "Maison Antoine" on Place Jourdan, "Frit Flagey" on Place Flagey and "Fritland" near Place de la Bourse.

Gaufre/Waffle

Belgian waffles are very popular all over the world. There are two types: Gaufre Liège and Gaufre Brussels.

The Liège version is a small round gaufre with a sugary consistency and is enjoyed without dressings.

The Brussels version is a square and crisp gaufre, with a soft and delicate taste inside. It is usually garnished with chocolate or fruit cream, whipped cream and much more.

In Brussels, one of the best places to enjoy gaufres is "Aux Gaufres De Bruxelles" a stone's throw from the Grand Place.

Moules marineère (steam mussels)

One of the main dishes of Belgian cuisine is the moules marineère, i.e. steamed mussels with white wine.

It is a simple dish of steamed mussels with celery and onions in white wine. Usually, a portion corresponds to one kilogramme of mussels, given the large waste of the shells of this dish.

Asparagus à la Flamande

If you visit Belgium in the spring, you should definitely try white asparagus specialties.

A classic dish is the asperges à la Flamande, served with boiled eggs and butter sauce.

Waterzooi

Waterzooi is a stew, originally from Flanders, in Ghent, in northern Belgium.

It is a chicken dish with egg cream. Originally the basic ingredients, were both river fish and sea fish. Later, it became chicken-based, because it was considered less expensive than fish.

Carbonade Flamande

The Carbonade Flamande is a traditional Flemish dish of stewed beef in beer with laurel, thyme, mustard and other spices. One of the best to taste in Brussels is at the restaurant "Le Clan des Belges" in Ixelles.

Boulet à la Liégeoise

This dish is native to the city of Liège. It is one or two meatballs (based on ground beef, pork and veal, onions, parsley and breadcrumbs) that are cooked in a dark sauce. They also combine Liège syrup and Corinthian raisins. This sauce is obtained, boiling onions, vinegar, cane sugar, apples, pears and sage.

Brussels sprouts

Brussels sprouts are a particular form of cabbage, originating in the capital of Belgium. They were named so because it is a vegetable cultivated and developed in the outskirts of Brussels in the seventeenth century. They are enjoyed in winter and can be both boiled and fried, and are often added as a side dish to meat dishes.

Anguilles au Vert (green eel)

Les anguilles au vert are a dish in which small pieces of eel are boiled for a long time with finely chopped herbs such as parsley, thyme, chives, basil, oregano, etc.

Chicon au jambon (Endive&Ham)

Chicon au jambon (Endive&HAm), is a dish eaten mainly in autumn and winter, due to the seasonality of the endive. The endive with the wrapped ham, is cooked in béchamel sauce and cheese.

Tomates Crevettes à la belge

In Belgian cuisine, grey shrimps caught in the North Sea are often used. These small shrimps are called crevettes. Famous as a Belgian appetiser, the tomates aux crevettes, consist of a bowl of tomatoes and filled with shrimp and mayonnaise.

Croquette de Crevettes

The creamy croquettes of Belgium, also contain shrimps of the North Sea.

Filet américain

The American fillet is a beef or horse steak in the Belgian style. It is made by adding mayonnaise and spices to raw meat. Unlike French tartar steak, it is seasoned with Belgian-style mayonnaise, onions, capers and Worcestershire sauce.

Gueuze or Kriek rabbit

Rabbit meat dish cooked in Gueuze or Kriek. The rabbit meat is left to marinate in vinegar, green pepper and beer for at least four hours.

Brussels: geography and historical notes

Geography and municipalities

The Brussels-Capital Region consists of 19 municipalities: Anderlecht, Auderghem, Berchem-Sainte-Agathe, Bruxelles-Ville, Etterbeek, Evere, Forest, Ganshoren, Ixelles, Jette, Koekelberg, Molenbeek-Saint-Jean, Saint-Gilles, Saint-Josse-Ten-Noode, Schaerbeek, Uccle, Watermael-Boitsfort, Woluwe-Saint-Lambert and Woluwe-Saint-Pierre.

For convenience in the book, the entire Brussels-Capital region is simply called Brussels.

Brussels is the most densely populated region in Belgium, and although it has the highest GDP per capita, it has the lowest available income per household. The Brussels Region covers 162 km2 (63 sq. miles), a relatively small area compared to the two other regions, and has a population of over 1.2 million. About 30 % of the total population is foreign, a quota that is constantly growing. There are 179 different nationalities, only Abu Dhabi (United Arab Emirates) counts more.

The five times larger metropolitan area of Brussels comprises over 2.5 million people, which makes it the largest in Belgium. It is also part of a large conurbation extending towards Ghent, Antwerp, Leuven and Walloon Brabant, home to over 5 million people.

Brussels is the capital of the Kingdom of Belgium but is also the de facto capital of the European Union as the seat of several institutions, including the European Commission, the European Council, the Council of the

European Union and, partially, the European Parliament (officially based in Strasbourg). Evere is also home to NATO headquarters.

The best museums/attractions to visit:

- Atomium
- Autoworld
- BOZAR
- Home of European History
- Belgian Cartoon Centre
- Mini-Europe
- Royal Museums of Fine Arts of Belgium
- Museum of Natural Sciences
- Museum of Musical Instruments
- Royal Museums of Art and History — Cinquantenaire Museum
- Royal Museum of the Army and Military History
- Royal Museum for Central Africa (in Tervuren)
- Parlamentarium

For more information:

- https://www.visit.brussels/en/visitors
- https://www.visitflanders.com/en

Historical notes

The date of origin of the town's settlement is not known with certainty. Excavations have revealed that the site has successively housed a Neolithic settlement, Roman villas and Merovingian farms.

The area became known around 580 AD when the Bishop of Cambrai built a chapel on an island of the Senne River. Around this chapel a community which was called "Broeksele" was created.

The official date of the city's foundation is 979 AD, when the Count of Brabant built a fortress by order of the Holy Roman Emperor, Otto II, (Otto the Bloody).

The agglomeration, populated by artisans and shopkeepers, passed under the dominion of the Counts of Leuven. One of them, Lamberto II, put in place an important project of walls whose construction took half a century. Over the same period, the Counts abandoned their old residence (Castrum) and settled in their new castles, built on the heights of Coudenberg (the actual Royal Square).

Brussels became a real city, since to enter it was necessary to pass through one of the seven gates. A true city that gradually achieved a political status, as it gave space to the sovereigns, who became dukes of Brabant, and for the patrician bourgeoisie.

The power of this bourgeoisie is symbolised by the honorific title of Duke. John II granted each of the seven descendants the privilege of possessing the key to one of the seven gates of the first walls.

Finished in 1379, the second walls follow the traces of the current boulevards of Petite Ceinture. The medieval period was characterised by numerous civil struggles between the population and its sovereigns.

In 1355, Duke John III died without male heirs and the Count of Flanders, Louis of Maele, took advantage of the situation to occupy the city. The domain was short-lived as two months later an army of Duchess Joan and her husband, Wenceslas of Luxembourg, took possession of the city.

During their reign, and more precisely in 1402, the first stone of the Hôtel de Ville was laid. The death of Duchess Giovanna at more than 80 years old, marked the end of the House of Louvain and the advent of the House of Burgundy.

For a quarter of a century, marked by civil and dynastic struggles, three Burgundians succeeded at the head of the Duchy. In 1430, the city and Brabant were under the dominion of Philip the Good. A period of great economic progress with the city that was characterised by the production of luxury goods.

The Burgundians unified all the Low Countries and Brussels became the seat of a lavish court.

At the end of the XV Century, Charles V ascended to the throne. He found himself King as of the Low Countries, also of Spain, Naples and Sicily on the paternal side; while on the maternal side Emperor of the Holy Roman Empire as his grandfather's legacy.

Charles V made Brussels the capital, and settled in the palace of the Coudenberg. In this way, despite the hostility of Malines, the city established its political and administrative pre-eminence at the head of the Low Countries and its economic growth accelerated.

Later the city adhered to the cause of William of Orange in a fierce struggle with Calvinism that ended only in 1585.

Despite a timid revival during the reign of the Archdukes Albert and Isabelle, during the 16th and 17th centuries, Brussels declined somewhat with Spanish Hapsburgs, without its role as the capital of the Spanish Low Countries being challenged.

Between 13 and 14 August 1695, the armies of Louis XIV, commanded by Marshal of Villeroy, bombed Brussels and several buildings were destroyed. It took four years to rebuild the Grand-Place.

When the Habsburg regime of Austria replaced that of their Spanish cousins in 1716, the city was in the grip of numerous incidents of social unrest. These ended three years later with the beheading of Dean of the Nation of St. Christopher, one of the Guilds of Brussels, François Anneessens. Traumatised, Brussels would have to wait 25 years before finding balance. The government of Charles of Lorraine led the city out of chaos and to the benefits of significant urban transformation.

At the dawn of the French Revolution, a third of the city's layout was entirely remodelled.

Brussels did not escape the philosophical-political turmoil that affected Europe at the end of the 18th century. Influenced by the ideas of the Enlightenment, Emperor Joseph II promulgated a series of reforms. The intentions were damaged by clumsy implementation. Resistance made its way in the spirit of the people. When Paris rebelled in 1789, Brussels would only remember the notion of insurrection against the foreigner. This all unfolded due to the defence of the ancient privileges of the Catholic Church and the bourgeois aristocracy.

Later, for one last time, stifled by the revolt of the population of the Low Countries, the Habsburgs were forced to step aside before the French Directory. After the Battle of Waterloo and the fall of Napoleon, Brussels, along with The Hague, became one of the two capitals of the new Kingdom of the Low Countries.

The Revolution of 1830, the independence of Belgium, and the rejection of the Dutch regime was a decisive and irreversible stage in the rise of Brussels to a great world city.

Belgium officially gained its independence on 21 July 1831 when the first King of the Belgians, Leopold I ascended the throne. Brussels was declared the capital of the kingdom.

During the rule of Leopold I, there was a long period of reconstruction, the city walls were demolished to allow urban renewal and city expansion. Several international congresses were organised, several scientific organisations were founded, as if to highlight their independence and a new importance in the international chessboard. During this period, foreign artists, philosophers and scientists, including Karl Marx and Victor Hugo, stayed in Brussels.

From this moment on, the city quickly acquired all the attributes of a modern city; the transformation of urban walls into boulevards, the construction of railway stations (the first dating back to 1835), the creation of a university in 1834, the distribution of drinking water at home, the of laying a sewage system, the realisation of ambitious urban projects, including the diversion of the Senne, which was not only a work for public health, but also an opportunity to give the boulevards of the centre the uniform aspect they still have today.

By concentrating an increasing number of administrative, commercial and financial activities in its centre, the city gradually absorbed the surrounding municipalities.

In the 20th century, Brussels suffered considerable damage during World War II, but once the Nazi occupation ended, the city continued its development process. In 1970, Belgium was divided into three autonomous regions, each with its own government; Flanders, Wallonia and Brussels-Capital. The city has become the de facto capital of the European Union and also of NATO, of which Belgium is a founding member.

How to get to Brussels

Brussels is at the centre of Europe and has important air, road and rail connections. More than 60 million Europeans live less than 300 km from Brussels, less than two hours by high-speed train. For those arriving by plane, the airport is 20 minutes away from the city centre. And once you get there, it's easy to get around the city, either on foot or by public transport.

By Train

Brussels Stations

National Society of the Belgian Railways (SNCB) www.belgiantrain.be

Five major stations serve the Brussels-Capital Region, all connected to each other.

The big stations:

• Brussels Centrale Carrefour de l'Europe 2-1000
• Gare du Midi rue de France 2-1070
• Gare du Luxembourg place du Luxembourg - 1040
• Gare Schuman rond-point Schuman - 1040
• Gare du Nord rue du Progrès 85 -1210

By Plane

Two airports serve the city; Brussels Airport and Brussels South Charleroi Airport.

Brussels Airport

Brussels International Airport is located to the northeast of the city, about 15 kilometres from the centre, in the municipality of Zaventem. Getting to the centre of the Belgian capital is very simple, thanks to the number and frequency of public transport.

Train

The train is the best way to get to Brussels from the airport: on floor -1 of the terminal is in fact the railway station, and the trains are frequent, clean and punctual. By train you can then continue to the cities of Ghent, Bruges or Antwerp, or change to Brussels Midi and board international high-speed trains, which travel to France, Germany and the United Kingdom.

. Trains leave every few minutes to numerous places in Belgium. The journey times are as follows.

- Central Brussels: 17 minutes
- Antwerp: 32 minutes
- Bruges: 90 minutes
- Charleroi: 83 minutes
- Ghent: 54 minutes
- Liège: 60 minutes
- Leuven: 15 minutes
- Mechelen: 15 minutes
- Namur: 72 minutes

For more information, you can visit the official website of the Belgian railways, where you can consult the updated timetables and buy the ticket. It is necessary to enter 'Brussels Airport' as a departure station and select the date of travel.

Alternatively, it is possible to buy the ticket directly at the station, to the automatic machines paying by ATM or credit card. The price of the single ticket is EUR 9.30.

Bus

It is also possible to arrive in Brussels by bus, via the STIB Airport Line, which includes line 12 (daily, direct) and line 21 (night, same route as line 12 but makes intermediate stops at different points of the city) of the public service. With the price of the EUR 7 ride, the bus is the cheapest way to get to the centre, but sometimes you have to deal with the city traffic. Again, some bus lines departing from Zaventem Airport travel national and international routes.

On the ground floor of Brussels Zaventem Airport, there is the bus station, where many companies stop. De Lijn and STIB are the two that make the connection to the city centre.

De Lijn operates connections between Brussels airport and Brussels-North railway station (lines 272 and 471), Roodebeek metro station (lines 359 and 659), and Expo district (line 820).

Taxi

Finally, if you are in a hurry or are looking for maximum comfort, you can arrive downtown using one of the many taxis ready to wait for you at the exit. The price of a ride to the centre is about EUR 45. Taxis are regulated by the taximeter and there is no fixed rate.

At Brussels Zaventem Airport, in front of the arrivals area, there is a parking lot for taxis. Brussels municipality taxis are easy to distinguish, as they are black with a yellow chessboard running along the side of the car.

Uber

Uber is active in Brussels, as in many other European cities. Prices to and from the airport are slightly lower than taxi prices.

Car

The route by car from Brussels Airport to the city centre takes between 20 and 25 minutes, depending on traffic. The distance is about 15 kilometres and getting to the centre is simple, as just outside the airport area is the entrance to the A201 road. Following the directions, staying on the E40, you arrive directly to the east of the city.

Given the small size of Belgium, from Brussels Zaventem Airport you can easily reach (traffic permitting) the main cities of the country:

• Antwerp: 30 minutes, 40 kilometers
• Ghent: 45 minutes, 65 kilometers
• Bruges: 1 hour and 10 minutes, 110 kilometres
• Charleroi: 45 minutes, 70 km
• Liège: 1 hour, 90 kilometres

The airport is therefore an excellent starting point for an on the road tour to discover Belgium, or the Flanders region.

Brussels South Charleroi Airport

Charleroi Brussels International Airport is located south of the city, at a distance of about 50 kilometres. Although the distance is not short, getting to the centre of Brussels is quite easy. This airport has had significant growth in the last decade thanks to low-cost airlines.

Bus

To get from Charleroi Airport to the centre of Brussels, the best option is the Brussels City Shuttle: a bus operating the route from the airport to Brussels Midi train station, every 30 minutes from 3:30 a.m. until midnight. To get the best price you need to book online well in advance. The cost of the route is 15.5 if bought online and 17 if bought at the airport.

The bus for the return journey from Bruxelles Midi to Charleroi Airport departs from outside the station, at the intersection of Rue de France and Rue de l'Instruction. In this case, it is possible to buy the ticket directly from the driver, but be careful, as the seats not booked online and still available are often very few. You may risk not being able to get on board, so if you can't make your tickets online, you will have to be at the stop well in advance, considering that you might miss a bus or two.

Train

TEC (Transport En Commun) operates urban public transport in the Belgian region of Wallonia. The urban bus line A, operated by TEC, connects from Charleroi-Brussels South Airport to Charleroi railway station. The ticket is purchased directly on board, or at automatic machines outside the airport.

Once you arrive at the Charleroi train station, you can take advantage of the Belgian railway system to move around the country in complete autonomy.

Taxi

At the exit of the terminal there is the parking lot for taxis. There are several private taxi companies that have permission to collect passengers at Charleroi airport. Although the price list is not the same for all companies, the price of a ride to and from Brussels is fixed, and is around EUR 85. Taxis can accommodate up to 4 people, but for trips up to 8 people you can reserve a minibus.

Car

A rental car is a great way to get to Brussels and move around in the following days.

The route by car from the terminal to the centre of the Belgian capital lasts about 45 minutes, with normal traffic, and, first along the A54 and then entering the A7, until the entrance into the city. The distance to be covered is less than 60 km.

Connections to Brussels Airport

There is no direct connection between Charleroi airport and Brussels Zaventem airport, however, it is certainly not difficult to travel independently: once disembarked, just board the Brussels City Shuttle, which leads directly to the Brussels-Midi train station. From there, there are numerous trains departing every hour to Zaventem Airport. The entire route lasts no more than an hour and 30 minutes, counting also the time for waiting for the vehicles.

Alternatively, the Intercity 4011 train departs every hour from Charleroi's city railway station, and in just over an hour and a half arrives at Zaventem Airport, making a series of intermediate stops. To get from Charleroi Airport to the train station, you need to take a taxi or use the scheduled bus, which run the route in just 20 minutes.

Getting around Brussels

Since January 2021, Brussels has been a 'City 30'. This means that the speed limit in the capital is 30 km/h for all road users. Exceptions to this rule are some large traffic axes (if the speed limit is 50 or 70 km/h, beware of road signs) and residential areas (speed limit: 20 km/h).

These speed limits apply to all road users (cars, vans, trucks, motorcycles, motorcycles, buses, bicycles, scooters, etc.). Only trams, rescue services and snow blowers are not subject to the speed limit.

Public transport

STIB, the Brussels Inter-municipal Transport Company, provides most public transport in the Brussels-Capital Region. The network includes metro lines that connect the east and west districts of the city. The "prémétro" lines (a kind of underground tramway) complete those of the metro. There are also numerous tram and bus lines on the surface. Check the timetables on the STIB website.

You can find free public transport maps at KIOSK counters, Bootik Information Offices

Real time to Metro from downtown (Da Brouckère):

- 7 mins: Schuman (European Quarter)
- 9 mins: Mérode (Fifteenth anniversary)
- 15 mins: Roodebeek (Woluwe Shopping Center)
- 14 mins: Louise (Shopping — Upper part of the city)
- 17 min: ROI Baudouin (Bruparck — Atomium)
- 19 mins: Herrmann-Debroux (Soignes Forest)

Where to buy a ticket?

• At the KIOSK counters in metro stations;
• At a GO automatic counter at some stops and at all stations;
• At the information desks of STIB;
• At numerous newsstands;
• At the reception office: Rue du Marché-aux-Herbes 63 • 1000 Brussels (only daily ticket).

Rates:

A single ride costs EUR 2.40. A booklet of 10 trips costs EUR 15.60 and a day ticket EUR 7.80.

Recently, the possibility to purchase via contactless directly in the car at a cost of 2.10 per ride has been added.

Every weekend, until 3:00 a.m., some bus lines cover the Brussels-Capital region.

City Card

The Brussels City Card is called the Brussels Card, and is a card designed specifically for tourists that allows free access to 49 museums and discounts for attractions, guided tours, shops and restaurants. With this purchase, you can also choose to combine the option of public transport, so you can use it to move around the city for free, including bus lines 12 and 21 to and from the airport.

The Brussels Card is available in 24-hour, 36-hour and 72-hour cuts.

Bicycle rental

Brussels is a "bike friendly" city with numerous bike paths.

Villo — bike rental at 350 points of the Brussels Region

Open 7 days a week and 24 hours a day, Villo! allows you to move freely both during the day and night. You can make an unlimited number of routes throughout the duration of your subscription, whether you are an occasional or regular user.

www.villo.be

On foot

In Brussels, walking routes have the advantage of always being very accessible. In general, I recommend seeing it as much as possible on foot.

Here are some examples:

• Louise district — Grand Place: 15 minutes
• Grand Place — European Quarter: 25 minutes
• European Quarter — Louise Quarter: 25 minutes
• Louise district — Marolles: 5 minutes
• Marolles — Grand Place: 10 minutes
GrandPlace — Sablon: 10 minutes
• Sablon — Forest of the Cambre: 40 minutes

Parking spaces

Practically, it is necessary to pay in every parking site. It is possible to buy the parking ticket online. For paid parking www.interparking.com

Where to stay in Brussels

Brussels, like all major European capitals, offers plenty of choice for overnight stays.

The reference sites are always the usual Booking.com and AIRBN.

I also recommend taking a look at the various B&Bs that are located in the city, often in residential neighbourhoods.

In general, I suggest avoiding hotels around the Gare du Nord and the Gare du Midi and recommend areas such as Louise and the city centre.

During the weekend, in the European neighbourhood hotels offer attractive prices (on the other hand you should avoid this area during the week).

Brussels with children

Travelling with kids is lovely but sometimes complicated.

Brussels is a city that loves children and families. They'll find so many things to do.

On public transport, there are spaces for strollers and most metro stations are equipped with lifts to reach the platforms.

The two airports offer a dedicated children's play area.

Belgians are used to going to bar with their children. So, you won't have any problems visiting bars and restaurants.

As far as city breweries, La Source is definitely the best equipped to accommodate the little ones by having a specific play area.

Beer Tour

Did you enjoy the book? Would you like to visit a brewery or participate in a beer tasting or food-beer matching event?

Write me an e-mail! beertastersbrussels@gmail.com

Bibliography

- Jackson, M., *Beer companion,* Duncan Baird Publishers, 1997

- Lacambre, G., *Traité complet de la fabrication des bières et de la distillation des grains,* Decq, 1851

- Stange, J., De Baets, Y., *Around Brussels in 80 Beers,* Cogan&Mater, 2009

- Symons, T., Lefebvre, S., van Praag, Y., *Estaminet et Cafès,* Bruxelles Frabiques, 2018

- Walsh E., *Brussels Beer City,* Amazon Fullfillment, 2019

- Walsh, E., *A history of Brussels Beer in 50 objects,* Amazon Fullfilment, 2022

- Webb, T., Stange, J., *Good Beer Guide Belgium,* CAMRA 2014

- Weber, P., *Bruxelles Omnibus,* Edition Michel Lafon, 2019

Acknowledgments

Writing a book is an adventure. Writing is like travelling. You travel in your mind at the rhythm, sometimes slow, sometimes unbridled, of your keyboard.

I would like to thank all the brewers who granted me an interview starting with a living beer legend in Brussels, Jean-Pierre Van Roy.

Thanks also to Yvan De Baets, Alexis Boisseau, Maxime Dumay, Sébastien Morvan, Nacim Nemu, Maxim Lagrillière, Arthur Ries, Mathieu Huygens, Christophe Bravin, Joel Galy, Jean Van de Broeck, Charles Grison, Edward Grison, Yorick Coomans, Emile Piret, Thomas Detourbe, Gilles Bastin, Mathieu Alan, Morane Le Hiress, Aylin Dirioz Fastenau, Daniel Fastenau, Manuel Moretto, Felix Bourée, Bart Van Leemput, Samuel Lange, Sébastien Cantineau, Gauthier Crèvecoeur, Michaël Boutriaux and Gregoire Malcause. Through their stories, and their beers, I experienced the past and present of Brussels berr scene. Through their ideas, I tried to imagine the future of this amazing city.

Thanks also to Jean Hummler, Grégoire Rifaut and Michael Eftekhari, leading actors of the rebirth of craft beer scene in the city.

Thanks also to Sven Gazt for sharing with me his vision, as a politician and beer lover, of the city in all its aspects.

Thanks to Patrick Larkin for proofreading the book.

Thanks to Andrea Turco, guru of Italian craft beer scene, for giving me the opportunity to be part of the editorial staff of Cronache di Birra (from which there is always so much to learn).

Thanks to all the friends in Italy and in Belgium with whom in recent years I have tasted many delicious Belgian beers and enjoyed fantastic evenings.

Thanks to my parents, Fabrizio and Clementina, and to my sister Beatrice, who have always pushed me to believe in what I do.

Thanks especially to Ilaria, the sweet patient other half of my life, for supporting all my projects.

And thanks to the little Vittoria Michela, whose smiles are the most important thing for a father who never wants to stop.

The Author

Niccolò Querci was born in Bergamo on September 7, 1987. He graduated in International Relations. He lives in Brussels since more than 10 years and he works with European funds related to research and innovation.

He obtained the qualification of Beer Sommelier at the Beer&Cider Academy in London, he is a member of the editorial staff of "Cronache di Birra" (the most important blog about craft beers in Italy), he is member of the British Guild of Beer Writers and founder of Beer Tasters Brussels through which he organises tastings, beer&food pairing and beer tours of Belgium.

Printed in Great Britain
by Amazon

56358314R00188